ARKY

Also by:

Arkansas at Work: 1900 to 1925
Steven Hanley

Arkansas County
Ray & Steven Hanley

Around Little Rock: A Postcard History
Ray & Steven Hanley

Camp Robinson and the Military on the North Shore
Ray Hanley

Carroll and Boone Counties
Ray & Diane Hanley

Hot Springs, Arkansas
Ray & Steven Hanley

Hot Springs, Arkansas, in Vintage Postcards
Ray & Steven Hanley

Hot Springs: Past and Present
Ray Hanley

Jonesboro and Arkansas' Historic Northeast Corner
Ray & Diane Hanley

A Journey through Arkansas Historic U.S. Highway 67
Ray Hanley

Little Rock Then and Now
Ray Hanley

Lost Little Rock
Ray Hanley

Main Street Arkansas: The Hearts of Arkansas Cities and Towns—
As Portrayed in Postcards and Photographs
Ray & Steven Hanley

Malvern
Ray & Steven Hanley

Newton County
Ray & Diane Hanley

A Place Apart: A Pictorial History of Hot Springs, Arkansas
Ray Hanley

Remembering Arkansas' Confederates
Ray & Steven Hanley

Sebastian and Crawford Counties
Ray & Steven Hanley

Washington and Benton Counties
Ray & Diane Hanley

Wish You Were Here
Ray & Steven Hanley

ARKY

The Saga of the USS *Arkansas*

The true story of a battleship that carried the state's name through
a Mexican invasion, two world wars, and into the dawn of the atomic age.

Ray Hanley and Steven Hanley

BUTLER
CENTER
BOOKS

The Butler Center for Arkansas Studies
Central Arkansas Library System
100 Rock Street
Little Rock, Arkansas 72201
www.butlercenter.org

First edition: February 2015

ISBN 978-1-935106-78-4
ISBN 978-1-935106-79-1 (e-book)

Manager: Rod Lorenzen
Book and cover design: H. K. Stewart
Copyeditor: Ali Welky

Library of Congress Cataloging-in-Publication Data

Hanley, Ray, 1951-
  Arky : the saga of the USS Arkansas / Ray Hanley, Steven Hanley.
    pages cm
  Includes bibliographical references and index.
  ISBN 978-1-935106-78-4 (pbk. : alk. paper) — ISBN 978-1-935106-79-1
(e-book) 1. Arkansas (Battleship) 2. World War, 1939-1945—Naval
operations, American. 3. World War, 1914-1918—Naval operations,
American. 4. Operation Crossroads, Marshall Islands, 1946. I. Hanley,
Steven G., 1952- II. Title. III. Title: Saga of the USS Arkansas.
  VA65.A79H36 2015
  359.8'352—dc23
                                        2014035896

Printed in the United States of America
This book is printed on archival-quality paper that meets requirements of the
American National Standard for Information Sciences, Permanence of Paper,
Printed Library Materials, ANSI Z39.48-1984.

Butler Center Books, the publishing division of the Butler Center
for Arkansas Studies, was made possible by the generosity of Dora
Johnson Ragsdale and John G. Ragsdale Jr.

*Dedicated to the thousands of servicemen
who went to sea in the service of the United States
aboard the USS Arkansas between 1912 and 1946*

Acknowledgements

This book, with stories and many photos never before in print, was made possible by the contributions of a number of people. They include Michael Pocock of the Maritime Institute; David Colamaria of the Steel Navy website; Dave Roberts, who shared his father's WWII journals; Annette Knipfing; A. A. Sirco, who shared his *Arkansas* journal that spanned both the European and Pacific theaters of war; Calline Ellis of Fort Smith for sharing the WWII memories of Dr. Homer Ellis; James Elliott, William Ringgold, and Jack Freeze for sharing their memories of sailing the *Arkansas* to its fate at the Bikini Atoll; Diane Hanley for editing help; and, lastly, Cathy Bain for her patient technical assistance whenever computer expertise was needed at odd hours of the night.

A special thanks also goes to Jonathan Weisgall, who as a young attorney helped win some justice and compensation for the people of the Marshall Islands affected by the atomic bomb tests, and who graciously gave me permission to quote from his wonderful book, *Operation Crossroads*, about the bomb tests that sank the USS *Arkansas*. After a four-year effort to develop this book, I'd also like to thank Rod Lorenzen of Butler Center Books for finding a way to get it into print, H.K. Stewart for designing the final work you hold in your hands, and Ali Welky also of Butler Center Books for an outstanding editing job.

Contents

Foreword 11

CHAPTER ONE
First Arkansas Namesake Warships:
One Grey, One Blue, One of a Nation United 15

CHAPTER TWO
A New Warship That Would Make History 20

CHAPTER THREE
First Combat 35

CHAPTER FOUR
Training to Join a World at War. 44

CHAPTER FIVE
Between the Wars 56

CHAPTER SIX
D-Day Heroism 83

CHAPTER SEVEN
War in the Pacific. 110

CHAPTER EIGHT
Sacrificed to the Dawn of the Atomic Age 130

Afterword. 155

Notes 157

Bibliography. 161

Index 165

Foreword

While on the Arky, we survived many enemy attacks on both the Atlantic and Pacific Oceans. Frightening as these attacks were, some of the scariest moments I recall were not threats brought on by the enemy, but by Mother Nature.

"Permission to come aboard, Sir!" These were the first words I said as I stepped onto the teakwood deck of the USS *Arkansas* in August 1943. Thus began an adventure of two and a half eventful years. When we parted, I went on to enjoy a long life, though the "Arky" was not so fortunate.

Prior to World War II, the Arky was slated to be dismantled and sold for scrap. The Japanese were eager to buy all the metal they could, which they molded into all kinds of armaments. They soon gave the metal back to us, beginning with the attack at Pearl Harbor.

While on the Arky, we survived many enemy attacks on both the Atlantic and Pacific Oceans. Frightening as these attacks were, some of the scariest moments I recall were not threats brought on by the enemy, but by Mother Nature. One such event happened in the North Atlantic when, during a storm, I was hit by a wave and was almost washed overboard. Luckily, I was able to grab on to a lifeline until the Arky managed to right herself. I then ran up to the bridge, this being the only way to get to safety below deck since all other hatches had been battened down. As I raced to the bridge, I remember someone saying to me, "You're as white as a sheet!" My heart was pounding and I was literally shuddering with fear.

All ships have some degree of inclination, so that when a certain tilt is reached, the ship will roll over and likely sink. One time during rough seas, the Arky came within three degrees of that point. When the good old Arky began to right herself, a great chorus of "Hoorahs" was heard amongst the crew, not to mention several "Amens."

I recall another fearful moment while riding out a typhoon in the Pacific. With air attacks, we had several means of defense, but this is not so against the fury of Mother Nature. Our only hope of defending ourselves from the turbulent sea was to steer the ship directly into the oncoming wave; to be caught parallel to a trough could be fatal. As with every battle before, the Arky sailed through this storm to see another day. Sadly, other ships were not so fortunate; the United States lost three destroyers in this same storm, and I believe all hands were lost.

Friendships were an important part of our lives on board. My division had about thirty crewmen, and, as often as not, close friendships occurred between a few of them. Whenever possible, we went ashore together to see the sights, visit museums, and patronize a local bar or two. Once, when docked in Taranto, Italy, I went ashore with two of my friends, both of whom were of Italian descent and spoke a smattering of the language. While in town, we met a native Italian sailor whose father owned a local vineyard. He took us to his wine cellar where, after a few hours of getting acquainted, we became the poster picture of drunken sailors.

While we partied, French naval ships had also anchored in Taranto. At that time, the French and Italians had a long-standing feud, accusing each other of introducing syphilis into their respective cultures. As my group emerged from the wine cellar, we unknowingly stumbled into a small-arms firefight between French and Italian sailors. We quickly retreated to the safety of the wine cellar to avoid injury.

Having seen duty in the European theater and then in the Pacific, at war's end we sailed to Seattle, back in the good old USA. On my final departure from the Arky in February 1946, I paused one last time to salute and said, "Permission to go ashore, Sir!"

Once back in the States, promises of reunions and continuing friendships never materialized for me. I was reintroduced to my pre-war life, and going to school on the GI Bill left little time for anything else. Eventually, the sameness and routine of everyday life began to bore me. My time on the Arky had changed my outlook on life, so after a year of civilian life, I joined the U.S. Air Force. I was sent to Fort Worth, Texas, where I—a Yankee—met and married a beautiful Texas girl (who had said "never the twain shall meet"!). Together, we traveled to many places in the United States and overseas, and we had four children, each one born in a different state or country. We've been married now for over sixty years and have five grandchildren, with six great-grandchildren on deck and two below deck.

These days, I am astounded by the number of Americans who are still ignorant of the history surrounding World War II, even the events at Pearl Harbor. I believe it was George Santayana who first said, "Those who cannot remember the past are condemned to repeat it." Of course many years have passed, and some recollections of my days on the old Arky have dimmed, as time has a way of affecting memories.

What I do know is that the Arky is gone, and only a few of us who knew her are still here.

I wish to thank Ray and Steven Hanley for their tireless efforts of research, assimilation, and coordination in creating this work and helping to keep the memories of our past alive.

May God bless America!

Anthony A. Sirco, GM3/C
USS *Arkansas*

[Mr. Sirco passed away on March 20, 2013,
while this book was still in progress.]

Chapter One

First Arkansas Namesake Warships: One Grey, One Blue, One of a Nation United

Its life in service was but twenty-three days, it came to a fiery, violent end, and it flew the Confederate "Stars & Bars." Regardless of that history, the CSS *Arkansas* lays claim to being the first warship to carry the name of the state of Arkansas.

In the early months of the Civil War, the Confederacy knew it was going to be challenged to control the rivers, especially the Mississippi that flowed through the heart of the breakaway nation. Toward meeting that challenge, the Confederate navy ordered a pair of ironclad warships from a Memphis shipbuilder.

The Union naval force was bearing down on Memphis in April 1862 and the Confederate ironclad was still not finished. The *Arkansas* was towed south and up the Yazoo River in Mississippi, where the Confederates hoped it could be hidden and finished.

In May 1862, Lieutenant Isaac Brown arrived at the work site on the Yazoo River, where he hoped to find his assigned ship, the CSS *Arkansas*, ready for service. Lt. Brown found the ship far from ready. No armor had been affixed to the wooden framework, the engines were in pieces, and no gun carriages were mounted. Five more weeks of work would have the ship as ready as it could be made under the conditions. Ten guns were mounted and a complement of 232 men and officers was available for service.

By July 1862, it became apparent to Lt. Brown that he and the crew were going to have to move the *Arkansas*, as the level of the Yazoo River was falling dangerously low. Orders came to take the ship downriver in

The CSS Arkansas won the short battle, doing damage to the three Union gunboats, and was soon moving off the Yazoo River into the main channel of the Mississippi, where a much larger enemy fleet lay in wait.

defense of the key Mississippi River port of Vicksburg, under siege by the Union navy. The effort to be battle ready was threatened when a boiler leaked steam into the gunpowder storage compartment, making the powder too damp for use in the ship's guns. Time was lost in drying it out, but without usable gunpowder, the ship would have been without any ability to defend itself.[1]

The Union navy was waiting for the Confederate warship around a bend in the Yazoo. The battle would be short but bloody, as vividly detailed in Captain Samuel Harris's account. Capt. Harris commanded some fifty "Missouri Volunteers" who helped man the *Arkansas*. "The first blood was drawn from my division. An Irishman, with more curiosity than prudence, stuck his head out the broadside port, and was killed by a heavy rifle bolt which had missed the ship. Stevens was with me at the time; and, fearing the sight of the mangled corpse and blood might demoralize the gun's crew, sprang forward to throw the body out of the port, and called upon the man nearest to assist. 'Oh! I can't do it, sir,' the poor fellow replied. 'It's my brother.' The body was thrown overboard."[2]

The CSS *Arkansas* won the short battle, doing damage to the three Union gunboats, and was soon moving off the Yazoo River into the main channel of the Mississippi, where a much larger enemy fleet lay in wait. Against all odds, the Confederate ironclad plowed through some thirty Union warships with guns blazing and was soon headed into sheltered anchorage beneath the Confederate batteries of Vicksburg.

A week later, with partial repairs made to the extent that circumstances allowed, the *Arkansas* was ordered out of the protected anchorage of Vicksburg with the assignment to proceed downriver to attack Union-occupied Baton Rouge. The ship's commander, Lieutenant Isaac Brown, was absent at the time, receiving medical treatment in Grenada, Mississippi.[3]

Confederate commander General Earl Van Dorn, who ordered the ship to Baton Rouge, should have heeded the earlier advice of the absent Lt. Brown and delayed the ship's return to battle. Within sight of Baton Rouge and under the watch of the wary Union navy, the engines broke down on the *Arkansas*, leaving the ship with no means to maneuver. To prevent the ship from becoming a Union trophy of war, the crew grounded the ship and set it afire, fleeing ashore just before the ship exploded. Today, the remains of the storied CSS *Arkansas* rest beneath a Mississippi River levee in West Baton Rouge Parish; its captured flag is on display at the National Civil War Museum in Columbus, Georgia.[4]

The Confederate ironclad warship CSS Arkansas was rushed into service before it was even completed, in an effort to break the Union navy's siege of Vicksburg, Mississippi. Manned by almost 200 sailors and soldiers, the Arkansas frustrated the numerically superior Union navy for some three weeks in the summer of 1862, inflicting numerous casualties and damaging a number of the enemy's wooden ships.

Twenty-three days of glory for the CSS Arkansas would come to an explosive end near Baton Rouge. While the warship's seasoned commander was on leave, Confederate general Earl Van Dorn ordered the mechanically impaired ship out of Vicksburg to engage the enemy farther down the Mississippi. When its engines failed within sight of the enemy, the crew set the ship afire and abandoned the vessel, which soon exploded—to the cheers of nearby Union forces. It rests today deep beneath a Mississippi River levee.

*The third warship to bear the name of the state of Arkansas was put to sea in 1900—less than forty years after the Civil War ended—to serve the **U.S. Navy. The USS** Arkansas was one of four single-turreted monitor-class warships first built for the navy in the late 1800s.*

As dramatic as the saga of the Confederate CSS *Arkansas* is in the history books, there was, by comparison, an almost totally overlooked Union naval vessel that also carried the name of the state of Arkansas. The wooden ship was launched in 1863 with the name *Tonawanda* before being purchased by the Union navy to be retrofitted as a warship. For reasons not clear, although perhaps recalling the heroic CSS *Arkansas*, the ship was christened the USS *Arkansas* and manned with an eighty-six-member crew. The ship's service would consist largely of blockade duty in the Texas Gulf Coast and around the mouth of the Mississippi River below New Orleans. The USS *Arkansas* survived the Civil War to be decommissioned and sold at public auction in July 1865. The ship's coastal merchant work was ended abruptly when it sank in March 1866 after becoming stranded on Grecian Shoals off the coast of Florida.[5]

The third warship to bear the name of the state of Arkansas was put to sea in 1900—less than forty years after the Civil War ended—to serve the U.S. Navy. The USS *Arkansas* was one of four single-turreted monitor-class warships first built for the navy in the late 1800s. The new ship, powered by coal for its steam engines, maintained a crew of 220 upon commissioning. Part of this crew would maintain the bunker of 350 tons of coal needed to feed the ship's four boilers, powering its 2,400-horsepower engines. These engines could drive the 255-foot-long ship through the water at a speed of twelve knots an hour.

The low-profile vessel was designed to offer little surface image in order to make its detection harder for enemy ships. The stealth design would not be needed, however, as the ship would spend its career on training and coastal patrol duty without ever firing a shot in combat. With the start of construction on a new modern battleship in 1909, the *Arkansas* was renamed the USS *Ozark*. The ship was decommissioned and sold for scrap metal in 1922.[6]

The first monitor-class U.S. Navy ships—essentially iron-hulled, twin-screwed craft—were primarily intended for coastal defense. One of the last of the type to be put to sea was the USS Arkansas, launched on November 10, 1900. The vessel, powered by steam, was 255 feet long and weighed more than 3,000 tons. The Arkansas carried a crew of 220 enlisted men and officers.

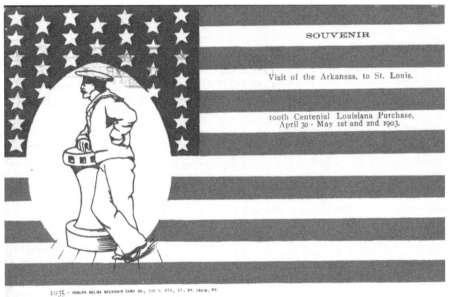

SOUVENIR

Visit of the Arkansas, to St. Louis.

100th Centenial Louisiana Purchase,
April 30 - May 1st and 2nd 1903.

1035 - ADOLPH SELIGE SOUVENIR CARD CO., 106 N. 4TH, ST., ST. LOUIS, MO

The early years of the USS Arkansas service were spent in training the midshipmen of the Naval Academy, but it saw other waters as well. The shallow draft of the ship, some twelve feet, allowed it to ply the Mississippi River to attend the centennial of the Louisiana Purchase in St. Louis in 1903. When construction on a new, modern USS Arkansas began in 1909, the ship was renamed the Ozark. The vessel served shore patrol in the Gulf of Mexico during World War I and would be sold for scrap in 1922.

Chapter Two

A New Warship That Would Make History

The battleship that would often be referred to during World War II as the "Arky" was under construction by the end of the first decade of the twentieth century. The third USS *Arkansas*, the B-33 (as the navy had begun to number its new ships), was christened by Nancy Macon, daughter of Arkansas congressman Robert B. Macon, on January 14, 1911. A period of more than a year and a half of fitting out was required to ready the new warship for duty. The *Arkansas* was finally commissioned on September 17, 1912, at the Philadelphia Naval Yard.

Captain Roy Campbell Smith, an 1878 Naval Academy graduate, was the new battleship's first commander. At the Battle of Santiago during the Spanish-American War in 1898, he served on the USS *Indiana*. He was awarded the Navy Cross and other decorations for service in that conflict.[1]

The commissioning of the USS *Arkansas* was indirectly responsible for the creation of the official state flag of Arkansas. When the Pine Bluff chapter of the Daughters of the American Revolution (DAR) decided to present the newly commissioned battleship with an American flag, a naval battalion ensign, and an official state flag, Arkansas secretary of state Earle W. Hodges informed the DAR that no official state flag existed. The organization launched a statewide contest to design one. Hodges agreed to chair the committee charged with selecting the winning design.

Sixty-five designs were submitted. The committee chose a red, white, and blue design submitted by Willie K. Hocker, a teacher and school principal in the Jefferson County rural community of Wabbaseka. With minor modifications in her original design, the banner is still in use today.[2]

The USS *Arkansas*, the second of two *Wyoming*-class battleships, was a near-sister of the USS *Florida*, as well as the USS *Texas*, USS *Utah*, and USS *New York*. These new American "dreadnoughts" were designed to win sea battles through superior firepower and speed. Measuring 562 feet by 93 feet, the *Arkansas* was armed with a dozen twelve-inch guns, each with a 16,000-yard range. The ship's secondary battery consisted of twenty-one five-inch/fifty-one-caliber guns protected by armor around the vessel's superstructure. Below the waterline were two twenty-one-inch torpedo tubes. Designed for a 1,594-man crew, and powered by newly developed coal-burning steam turbines, she had a top speed of twenty-one knots (approximately twenty-four mph).[3]

The new warship took part in a fleet review by President William Howard Taft in the Hudson River off New York City, receiving a visit from the portly chief executive on October 14, 1912. She then transported President Taft and his entourage to the Panama Canal Zone for an inspection of the unfinished waterway. After putting the presidential party ashore, the *Arkansas* sailed to Cuban waters for shakedown training. This regimen included battery practice and speed training, firefighting exercises, and seamanship drills. She returned to the Canal Zone on December 26 to carry President Taft to Key West, Florida.[4]

The battleship next joined the Atlantic Fleet for maneuvers along the East Coast. She began her first overseas cruise in late October 1913, visiting several Mediterranean ports. At Naples, Italy, on November 9, the ship celebrated the birthday of Victor Emmanuel III, King of Italy, firing her guns in a salute to the king and a host of Italian dignitaries who came aboard. The USS *Arkansas*'s crew would soon see combat for the first time.

These new American "dreadnoughts" were designed to win sea battles through superior firepower and speed. Measuring 562 feet by 93 feet, the Arkansas *was armed with a dozen twelve-inch guns, each with a 16,000-yard range.*

The hull of the fourth warship to carry the name of Arkansas was laid down in the Camden, New Jersey, shipyard on January 25, 1910. Over the next year, thousands of welders, electricians, and other workers would swarm over the 562-foot vessel taking shape as the USS Arkansas, intended to be a part of the nation's effort to modernize its navy. The USS Arkansas B-33 (as the navy was starting to number its ships) was launched from its covered berth on January 14, 1911. At its launch in the Camden shipyards, the Arkansas was not yet complete, but it was ready to float. It would be moved the short distance to the Philadelphia Naval Yard where the upper structure would be built and its guns installed.

Champagne-bottle launch honors were at the hands of Miss Nancy Louise Macon of Helena, Arkansas, on the day of her fifteenth birthday as the U.S. Navy's newest warship was christened with a bottle of champagne against her massive hull. The young lady was the daughter of Arkansas congressman Robert B. Macon, a lawyer and five-term congressman who would be defeated in 1913.

The USS Arkansas was commissioned at the Philadelphia Naval Yard on September 17, 1912, under the command of Captain Roy C. Smith. Assigned to the navy's Atlantic fleet, the ship, nearly the length of two football fields, was an imposing sight off the coast of New York. The 562-foot ship weighed over 27,000 tons, with a beam width of 93 feet and a draft (depth below the waterline) of 32 feet. The ship was armed with a dozen twelve-inch guns, twenty-one five-inch guns, and two submerged torpedo tubes.

The location is not noted, but the photo captured a group of sailors being ferried to the new USS Arkansas in 1912. The ship, slightly out of focus, is visible in the upper right corner of the photo. The black men in the photo, decades before the U.S. armed forces would integrate, are most likely employees of the ferry company transporting the sailors. Photo courtesy of Allen Whitwell of Pine Bluff, Arkansas.

On October 14, 1912, less than a month after being commissioned, the Arkansas took part in an Atlantic Fleet review before President William Howard Taft in the Hudson River off New York City. The president, who weighed some 300 pounds, is shown being escorted up the steps to the deck of the ship. Dressed in a long coat and a formal top hat, the commander-in-chief walked the deck followed by the ship's officers, all parading before the saluting enlisted men who lined the rail. A sailor aboard the ship penned on a photo, "The President dined with Ward Room. I had 8 p.m. to midnight in engine room."

Taft was defeated for reelection the next month by Woodrow Wilson. Taft, however, would make a return, longer visit to the Arkansas in December of 1912. The ship was tasked to carry Taft to visit the still uncompleted Panama Canal. Following the canal tour, the ship carried him to Key West Florida, where he would make a return to Washington DC by train.

The first to command the USS Arkansas, *from its commissioning in 1912 until October 1914, was Roy C. Smith. Under Captain Smith's lead, the* Arkansas *made its first trans-Atlantic trip in 1913, visiting Mediterranean ports, including Naples, Italy, where the ship participated in the birthday celebration of King Victor Emmanuel III.*

In December 1913, Rear Admiral Cameron Winslow, while commanding the U.S. Navy's First Division, was impressed enough with the Arkansas *to make it his flagship, passing over for the honor other ships under his command, including the* New York. *Admiral Winslow, born in 1854, lost his father to yellow fever in 1863 while his father was in command of the USS R. R. Cuyler during the Civil War. The younger Winslow graduated from the U.S. Naval Academy in 1874 and went on to become a decorated hero during the 1898 Spanish-American War. Under heavy enemy fire, Winslow cut two submerged cables off the coast of Cuba (getting shot through one hand in the process), cutting off Spain's military in Cuba from communication with Europe. The navy would later name a ship after him. He died in 1932.*

By the time the USS Arkansas was to be built, the U.S. Navy had accepted that coal-burning ships were much more efficient than the former steam-powered warships. While going full speed, a battleship like the Arkansas could burn eight to twelve tons of coal per hour. The work of making this coal available fell to the enlisted sailor. "Coaling a ship," as the work was known, was dirty, backbreaking work accomplished with hand shovels. As shown here, around the outbreak of World War I, the sailors of the Arkansas were loading the coal at dockside into containers that would be swung up and dumped into bins below deck. A good coal crew could move as much as 100 tons of coal an hour, and the commanders of the various ships competed to see whose sailors could move the most coal in the least time.

In a ca. 1915 edition of the Arkansas's news publication, the ship took credit for loading coal at a rate of 587 tons per hour. In 1918, with the Arkansas in European waters serving in World War I, a sailor, Z. C. Warren, wrote this from the ship home to Iowa: "I am always glad when we are through coaling the ship, for it sure is some dirty job, but, we do not mind it very much, for everyone on the ship has to work then." Photo courtesy of Maritime Quest from the Gilbert Holcomb Collection.

The clouds of coal dust added to an already steep hygiene challenge for enlisted sailors, who lacked the bathing facilities available to the officers of the ship. The men often bathed and did their laundry on the open deck of the Arkansas and its sister warships, as shown in this pre–World War I photo.

The massive coal-burning warships could not have come upon an enemy with stealth, as the great black clouds of dense smoke were visible for miles. Shown here, the Arkansas was in the lead of a group of the Atlantic Fleet in 1914. The ship would be converted to run on fuel oil in 1925.

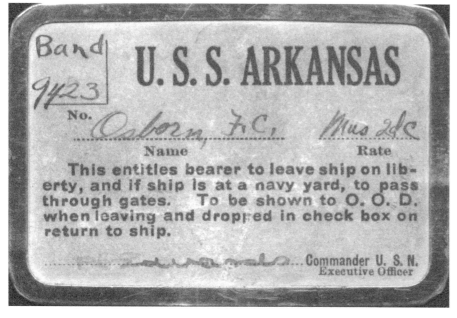

Obtaining an alcoholic drink became a lot harder for sailors in 1914. While it took until 1919 for the required two-thirds of states to vote to enact prohibition, the U.S. Navy acted five years earlier, banning beer and other alcoholic drinks from its bases and ships. The policy was ordered by Navy Secretary Josephus Daniels, who also issued orders that prostitution be banned within five miles of all U.S. Navy bases. As Prohibition was a U.S. social policy change, it was not binding in other nations, so controlling the USS Arkansas sailors' access to alcohol and other vices was a disciplinary challenge in the many foreign ports of call.

Shore leave was not granted liberally in the years before or during World War I. It was often used as a matter of discipline, as those sailors who worked hard and stayed out of trouble were most likely to be afforded a pass for a few hours' "R&R" while in a port of call. The one shown here was given around 1917, apparently to a sailor, F. C. Osborn, who was serving in the ship's band.

Some sailors sought to break the monotony of shipboard life by acquiring pets. These ranged from dogs and cats, sometimes kept under the title of mascots, to birds. The back of this ca. 1915 postcard read, "Mascot of the Arkansas saying 'get tell off the paint work.'" The parrot's name was Salvo, and, if he was like other talking birds who spent their time with sailors, he likely had a bit of a profane vocabulary.

As unlikely as it seems, at some point before World War I, the sailors had a bear aboard the ship, wearing a collar and some sort of uniform hat of one of the two men visiting on the ship in an unidentified port. The penned note on the card reads, "Arkies Three Bears, Joe Schilling, Bear, Amos."

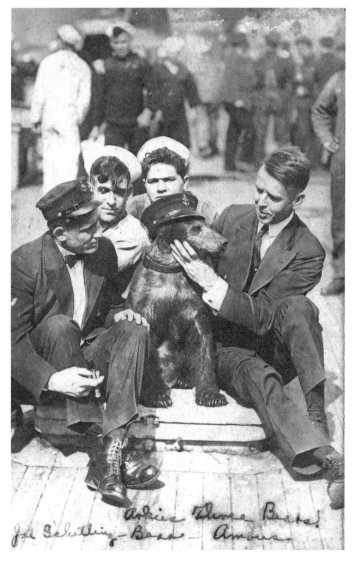

Gambling—by cards, dice, and other means—was a popular way to pass the time when consigned aboard the Arkansas. Others, perhaps between paydays, joined in other types of games. The sailors here were photographed around 1915 playing a game of acey deucey on the deck. The game, a variation of backgammon, originated in the Middle East.

Assigned initially to the east coast of the United States, the Arkansas *called most often on the ports of New York and the Brooklyn Navy Yard for repairs. The ship was photographed here before World War I in dry dock for repairs.*

The Arkansas, largest of Uncle Sam's War Vessels, in dry dock at the Brooklyn Navy Yards. World's target record, six hits in six shots in 57 seconds on Southern Drill Seas off Virginia Capes.

SEVENTY-FIRST YEAR

SCIENTIFIC AMERICAN

THE WEEKLY JOURNAL OF PRACTICAL INFORMATION

VOLUME CXII
NUMBER 6

NEW YORK, FEBRUARY 6, 1915

25 CENTS A COPY
$3.00 A YEAR

Copyright 1911 by Underwood & Underwood.

Tonnage, 26,000. Speed, 21 knots. Guns: Twelve 12-inch, twenty-one 5-inch. Torpedo tubes, 2. Belt armor, 11-inch. Maximum coal supply, 2,500 tons. Oil, 400 tons. Complement, 1,036.

THE UNITED STATES DREADNOUGHT "ARKANSAS"

The USS Arkansas was a favorite subject for popular magazines with the war already raging in Europe by 1915. Scientific American put the ship on the cover of its weekly publication on February 6, 1915. Noted across the bottom were features to impress potential magazine buyers and readers: "Tonnage, 26,000; Speed, 21 knots; Guns: twelve 12-inch, twenty-one 5-inch; Torpedo tubes, 2; Maximum coal supply, 2,500 tons; Oil, 400 tons; Complement, 1,036."

When on leave in the New York City ports, a popular stop for the sailors of the Arkansas was one of the local photographers who would make photo images of the dressed-up sailors on postcard stock that could be mailed back home. "U.S.S. Arkansas" is on a strip affixed to the front of the sailors' caps.

Chapter Three

First Combat

Tragically, this simple misunderstanding of men who did not speak the same language would provoke an international incident, leading to the deaths and injuries of hundreds of people.

In February 1913, Mexican general Victoriano Huerta overthrew his country's democratically elected president Francisco Madero, having him assassinated. Huerta then declared himself Mexico's military dictator. President Woodrow Wilson demanded that Huerta resign and allow free elections. The Mexican dictator rejected the ultimatum, and the stage was set for a military engagement by the United States that is today largely absent from the pages of the nation's history books.

On April 9, 1914, with the town of Tampico besieged by Constitutionalist forces, the commander of the USS *Dolphin* arranged for a purchase of oil from a warehouse near a tense defensive position at Iturbide Bridge. Nine U.S. sailors on a whaleboat flying the Stars and Stripes were dispatched to a warehouse. Seven of them brought the drums of oil back to the boat, while the other two stayed on board. Alerted to the activity, Mexican federal soldiers confronted the American sailors. Neither side spoke the other's language, thus the sailors did not respond to the commands of the soldiers. The Mexicans marched the Americans, including the two who had still been on the boat, to their nearby regimental headquarters; they were released unharmed less than two hours later. Tragically, this simple misunderstanding of men who did not speak the same language would provoke an international incident, leading to the deaths and injuries of hundreds of people.

Rear Admiral Henry T. Mayo, commanding the American Fleet, demanded a formal apology from Huerta's government for detaining the Americans, however briefly. The commander of the Tampico area, General Ignacio Zaragoza, offered a written apology; however, he steadfastly refused to raise the American flag on Mexican soil or provide a twenty-one-gun salute, both actions demanded by Admiral Mayo.

The next morning, Fletcher ordered additional sailors and marines to land, with the goal of occupying the entire city. The goal was aided when ships in the harbor, including the Arkansas, provided gunfire support.

President Wilson backed Mayo's demands. In a speech to a joint session of Congress, Wilson sought and obtained the authority to use military force in Mexico.[1] Although the provoking action of detaining the American sailors occurred in the city of Tampico, the target for the navy's fleet was the port city of Veracruz.

Warships of the United States' Atlantic Fleet under the command of Rear Admiral Frank Fletcher began preparations for the seizure of the city of Veracruz on the morning of April 21, 1914. By 11 a.m., the initial force of 500 marines and 300 sailors under the command of U.S. Navy captain William Rush landed at Pier 4. Meeting no resistance, the "blue-jackets" advanced, taking the customs house, post and telegraph offices, and railroad terminal while the marines moved to take the rail yard, cable office, and power plant.[2]

Fighting began when a local policeman, Aurelio Monfort, fired on the Americans; he was killed by return fire. Monfort's action led to wide-spread disorganized fighting. Arms were soon being distributed to the Mexican population, who were largely untrained in their use. Believing a large force was forming in the city, Captain Rush signaled for reinforcements. Sailors and marines from the USS *Utah* soon arrived. Seeking to avoid further bloodshed, Admiral Fletcher asked U.S. Consul William Canada to try to arrange a ceasefire. This effort failed when no Mexican leader came forward to negotiate.

Fletcher ordered Captain Rush to hold his position and remain on the defensive through the night. The USS *Arkansas* and four other battle-ships accompanied by two cruisers arrived that night, bringing reinforcements. The next morning, Fletcher ordered additional sailors and marines to land, with the goal of occupying the entire city. The goal was aided when ships in the harbor, including the *Arkansas*, provided gunfire support.

The marines, who had earlier filed off the *Arkansas* and other war-ships, quickly worked their way from building to building, shooting at Mexican soldiers and armed civilians. The Second Seaman Regiment, led by the USS *New Hampshire*'s Captain Edwin Anderson, headed up the Calle Francisco Canal. Upon being told that his line of advance had been cleared of snipers, Captain Anderson did not send out scouts, a mistake he would soon regret. Marching in parade formation, his men became easy targets for the cadets barricaded inside the Mexican Naval Academy. Three American warships in the harbor shelled the military school, silencing all resistance and killing fifteen cadets. Resuming their advance, the Second Seaman Regiment again came under sniper fire. Several men were lost. Artillery Commander John Grady of the USS *Arkansas* ordered cannon to be brought forward, and soon shells and shrapnel tore into the enemy position. The disheartened Mexican sharp-shooters surrendered when their position was overrun by bayonet-wielding naval infantrymen. By this time, gunfire was coming from the San Sebastian Hospital, over which the Red Cross flag was flying. The Americans stormed the medical facility, and six men surrendered on the roof. Another lay dead, sprawled beneath the Red Cross flag.[3]

Pockets of armed resistance continued, mostly in the form of hit-and-run guerrilla tactics, but within two days, all fighting ceased. Nineteen Americans had given their lives in the fighting and seventy-two had suffered combat wounds. Mexican losses were estimated at almost 200 killed, with an equal number wounded. The USS *Arkansas* contributed seventeen officers and 313 enlisted men under the command of Lieutenant Commander Arthur Keating. Bravery was on display among the *Arkansas*'s officers in the battles. Lieutenant junior grade Jonas Ingram would be awarded the Medal of Honor for heroism at Veracruz, as would Lieutenant John Grady, who commanded the artillery of the Second Seaman Regiment. Two *Arkansas* sailors paid the ultimate price, as Ordinary Seaman Louis O. Fried of Gretna, Louisiana, and Ordinary Seaman William L. Watson of Boston, Massachusetts, were killed. Seven *Arkansas* crewmen suffered combat wounds.

After four months service in Mexican waters, the USS *Arkansas* sailed to the U.S. Naval Station at Hampton Roads, Virginia, on October 7, 1914.[4]

Bravery was on display among the Arkansas's officers in the battles. Lieutenant junior grade Jonas Ingram would be awarded the Medal of Honor for heroism at Veracruz, as would Lieutenant John Grady, who commanded the artillery of the Second Seaman Regiment.

The USS Arkansas *saw its first combat supporting role in the spring of 1914, in what would have been considered an unlikely venue two years earlier when commissioned. President Woodrow Wilson, intent on blocking arms shipments to Mexican dictator Victoriano Huerta, ordered the navy off the port of Veracruz, Mexico. An apparent mistaken, but brief, detaining of Americans by Mexican officials was the final straw. Wilson ordered the navy to occupy the port city. Shown here are the landingcraft from the* Arkansas *(as denoted on the life rings), unloading sailors at the wharf of the Mexican city. Typed on the back of the postcard is: "The landing place, where the first shots were exchanged between our men and the natives."*

The invasion of Veracruz, without resistance initially, soon settled into a block-by-block battle. The Arkansas *contributed seventeen officers and 313 enlisted men to the invasion force. Some sailors, fearing their white uniforms would make them prime targets for Mexican snipers, dyed the uniforms in coffee and rusty water from the ship's boilers before coming ashore.*

The sailors' concerns about Mexican snipers were well-founded, as two from the Arkansas were fatally wounded in the streets of Veracruz. One of the men, either Ordinary Seaman Louis Fried or William Watson, is shown on a stretcher being rushed away from the heavy fighting. The men's bodies would be shipped back to New York City, where President Woodrow Wilson would attend their funerals.

The Mexican soldiers who battled the Americans in Veracruz paid a price in facing better-armed marines and sailors. Among the more than 200 Mexican forces killed was this Mexican soldier photographed where he fell.

"Sniper who killed Arkansas man shooting from window," is written on the photo, evidence that the killer of at least one of the Arkansas sailors was captured by American forces. The fate of the sniper once in custody was not recorded.

The marines and sailors had off-loaded small artillery pieces that were deployed when they met entrenched Mexican opposition.

Jonas H. Ingram, a graduate of the U.S. Naval Academy, was serving as the Arkansas's turret officer. He had previously established a world record for firing the twelve-inch (305mm) guns. The twenty-seven-year-old Ingram was awarded the Congressional Medal of Honor for his service in the Veracruz invasion. Ingram would later serve as the head football coach at the Naval Academy, win the Navy Cross in World War I, and become an admiral in World War II, during which he served in both the Atlantic and Pacific theaters of war.

It was perhaps the first such photo in American military history but one to be repeated over the next century far too many times, the result of armed conflict in far-flung regions of the world. The flag-draped caskets of some twenty U.S. servicemen, including two USS Arkansas sailors, were laid on the deck of the USS Montana for shipment home. Accounts of the Mexican dead and wounded ranged from 200 to 400, which included Mexican federal troops, civilians, and young cadets from a military academy.

The American forces would win the battle for Veracruz and fly the Stars and Stripes over the city, with the army soon taking over from the navy. The occupation lasted some four months, during which time the Arkansas remained in Mexican waters. A series of postcards of the events of the battles and occupation was created when the Arkansas's mail clerk R. M. Crosby hired a local Mexican photographer to produce the cards for Crosby to sell. The young man later used the profits to pay for his college tuition.

Captain Roy C. Smith was photographed on the deck of the Arkansas bestowing commendations for the action at Veracruz. In the aftermath of the fighting and occupation, navy secretary Josephus Daniels ordered the awarding of sixty-three Medals of Honor, the most for any wartime action before or since. One went to the army, nine to the marines and fifty-three to the navy.

The exploits of the USS Arkansas and her companion warships in the Mexican occupation were well covered by the press and helped the navy with its recruitment message. Among the promises were monthly pay between $17 and $77 a month, as well as board and lodging and medical care. Even the first uniform was promised free of charge.

*On January 20, 1917,
the* Arkansas *furnished
the Guard of Honor
for the funeral of
Admiral George
Dewey. Admiral
Dewey's victory on
May 1, 1898, at the
Battle of Manila Bay
during the Spanish-
American War had
destroyed the Spanish
Fleet without the loss
of a single man of the
American Fleet.*

Chapter Four

Training to Join a World at War

Its first combat ribbons awarded, the USS *Arkansas* was ordered to return to southern waters in January 1915 for further exercises. Upon completion of these, she sailed to Guantanamo Bay, Cuba, for fleet exercises. Returning to Hampton Roads, Virginia, in early April, the battleship began another training operation in the Southern Drill Grounds. On April 23, she headed back to the New York Navy Yard for two months of repair work. The warship left New York on June 25 bound for Newport, Rhode Island, where she conducted torpedo practice and tactical maneuvers in Narragansett Bay, Rhode Island, through late August.

Returning to Hampton Roads on August 27, 1915, the warship engaged in maneuvers in the Norfolk, Virginia, area through early October. The vessel carried out nine days of strategic exercises before sailing to the New York Naval Yard for dry-docking.

The *Arkansas* visited the West Indies and Guantanamo Bay before returning to the United States in March 1916 for a week of torpedo practice off Mobile Bay, Alabama. The battleship then steamed back to Guantanamo Bay, remaining there until mid-April when she once again dry-docked at the New York Naval Yard for overhaul.[1]

On January 20, 1917, the *Arkansas* furnished the Guard of Honor for the funeral of Admiral George Dewey. Admiral Dewey's victory on May 1, 1898, at the Battle of Manila Bay during the Spanish-American War had destroyed the Spanish Fleet without the loss of a single man of the American Fleet. He was the only person to have attained the rank of Admiral of the Navy, the most senior rank in the U.S. Navy.[2]

Throughout these years, the political scene across the sea in Europe continued to deteriorate. The winds of war blew strongly and soon swept the United States. On April 2, 1917, President Woodrow Wilson stood before a joint session of Congress adjusted his pince-nez spectacles, and told the nation: "The day has come when America is privileged to spend her blood and her might for the principles that gave her birth." Four days later, on Good Friday, the United States cast its lot with the Allies, entering the Great War against Germany.[3]

The declaration of war found the *Arkansas*—now attached to Battleship Division Seven—patrolling the mouth of the York River along the Atlantic coast of Virginia. For the next fourteen months, the vessel, now commanded by Captain W. H. G. Bullard, carried out routine patrol duty along the coast and trained gun crews for duty on armed merchantmen (merchant ships that carried guns). In July 1918, the *Arkansas* received orders to proceed to Rosyth, Scotland, to relieve the *Delaware*. With members of the House Naval Affairs Committee as passengers, the warship sailed on July 14.[4]

On the eve of her arrival in Rosyth, the *Arkansas* was churning through the frigid North Sea when a submarine periscope was sighted. Building up to her top speed of twenty-one knots, the battleship changed course, bringing the German U-boat astern. Captain Bullard ordered his number-two sky gun into action, and the obscure target was peppered with thirty-five rounds of blunt-nosed shell. The *Arkansas* swung hard to port to avoid an oncoming torpedo. The escorting destroyers dropped out of formation to administer depth charges. The *Arkansas*'s lookouts soon saw the periscope's wake disappearing in the distance. Without further incident, the warship dropped anchor at Rosyth on July 28, 1918.

One of the surviving accounts of a sailor aboard the *Arkansas* while engaged in WWI service was left by Z. C. Warren in a series of letters to Miss Ethel Hall of Carthage, Missouri, a young schoolteacher. Seaman Warren's letters were all stamped "censored" on the envelope, as they had presumably been read to ensure that he did not disclose anything that would endanger the ship in enemy waters if the letters were intercepted. In a letter dated June 12, 1918, Seaman Warren wrote to Ethel of the sensitive subject of cigarettes. "Please do not think hard of me for asking you to send me those cigarettes. I am now very sorry that I asked you to grant me this favor, for I see you are so bitterly opposed to them. I will have to agree with you in regards to the injury caused from them, but, you cannot imagine how much pleasure we are afforded out of our SMOKES."

He wrote: "Yes I am safe at this writing, and hope to remain safe, but you can never tell what will happen. Yes I understand that the German submarines are operating in the American waters, but, do not let that worry you. I don't think they will ever get to Carthage, Mo., do you? ... I had a letter from father yesterday, he said they had already

On the eve of her arrival in Rosyth, the Arkansas was churning through the frigid North Sea when a submarine periscope was sighted. Building up to her top speed of twenty-one knots, the battleship changed course, bringing the German U-boat astern. Captain Bullard ordered his number-two sky gun into action, and the obscure target was peppered with thirty-five rounds of blunt-nosed shell.

45

drafted 132 boys from my home town the 7th of this month, and were going to call for 100 more the 24th of July. This is a time we are going to have to pull together, for we are going to win this war, however it may take a long time, and may take a good deal of blood, but, Old Glory will finally be the flag of the victors, and she will now and forever wave, everyone must help, for we all have a part to play, and a sacrifice to make, maybe you have not brothers to go, [surely] you have a friend that has a brother or husband, and you hate to see them grieve, and you like everyone else will have to give up some of your worldly pleasures."

In a letter dated August 14, 1918, he wrote: "I have had the pleasure (if you want to call it that) of visiting Fritz in his back yard, but, unfortunately we did not get a chance to run him out, we had a little excitement, not very much. I sure will be glad when we have reached our goal, (VICTORY) that is a sweet name, and is worth fighting for, and I cannot help from believing that we are right, and that God is with us, and I am sure that we will place Old Glory, where she rightfully belongs, ABOVE ALL. Then we will come back to the dear ones we left behind." He wrote, "In Foreign Service, 24 September, 1918 It is cold 'Over Here,'" using a term evoking the phrase "Over There" that would become popular in story and song about the war.

By October, Seaman Warren—while still not disclosing locations—was writing Ethel of visiting ports in England and France while on shore leave. In a letter dated October 6, 1918, he wrote, "I am enclosing you a little handkerchief from 'OVER THERE.' I will send you some French magazines if you want them, but, you must first promise me that you will not get mad at me for sending them, you know they publish things that would make some of the Americans blush, and they sure do publish some real funny pictures....I sure do feel lonesome today but we have plenty to occupy our minds, and will look forward to the day that Germany is whipped, and from the looks of things now, the time is not very far off." Indeed, the war was but five weeks from ending, on November 11. On November 18, a week after the armistice, Seaman Warren wrote Ethel a long letter about the euphoria of the celebrations and also revealing a bit of his possible intentions toward her. He wrote: "I am feeling fine now, I think I have a right to feel good, since the war is over. I was in a large city the day after the armistice was signed. The Canadians, Australians, Scottish Highlanders and Americans sure had the city, I never seen anything like it in my life, they were doing a little bit of everything, marching, singing, hollering etc....Had a letter from Mother, there were a good many in Dickson died of the Flu, hope you escaped it." He was referring to the widespread influenza epidemic of 1918 that killed twenty million people around the world. "No indeed these girls 'over there' will never capture me, and I was not captured when we left the U.S. See, I am still 'at Large.' I have never thought very much about the 'Matrimonial Stuff' however I may change." Seaman Warren usually signed off to "Miss Ethel" as "Your friend, Z.C. Warren, U.S.S. Arkansas."

During the course of World War I, the battleship's newspaper the *Arklight* (sometimes spelled *Arklite*) began publication and was distributed to the crew. Its motto was printed as "Distemper Inemus," translated as "We Should Worry." At the close of the war, a book was compiled of poems the *Arkansas* crew had submitted to the paper while engaged in wartime service. The book *Comrades of the Mist* carried among its verses the following, poking fun at the Germans and boasting of the *Arkansas*.

SEA-GOING MOTHER GOOSE

Wilhelm had a little sub
He sent it out to sea,
And he told it to lie in wait
Where ships were sure to be.
It ran across the ARK one day,
We nailed it to the mast;

Poor Wilhelm hasn't many left,
He loses them so fast.[5]

Through the final three and a half months of the war, the *Arkansas*, along with five other U.S. battleships, remained stationed at Rosyth and operated as part of the British Grand Fleet as the Sixth Battle Squadron. The armistice ending World War I took effect on November 11, 1918. The Sixth Battle Squadron and other Royal Navy units were present at the surrender of the German Fleet at the Firth of Forth on November 21, 1918.

Released from service in the British Fleet on December 1, the American armada sailed to Portland, England, then out to sea to meet the transport *George Washington*, with President Woodrow Wilson on board. The *Arkansas*, along with other American battleships, escorted the president's ship to Brest, France. From there, Wilson would journey to Paris to attend the Paris Peace Conference at Versailles. Departing France, the *Arkansas* sailed to New York City, arriving on December 26, 1918, to a tumultuous welcome from throngs at dockside cheering the returning victors. Secretary of the Navy Josephus Daniels reviewed the assembled battleships from the yacht *Mayflower*.[6]

Released from service in the British Fleet on December 1, the American armada sailed to Portland, England, then out to sea to meet the transport George Washington, with President Woodrow Wilson on board. The Arkansas, along with other American battleships, escorted the president's ship to Brest, France. From there, Wilson would journey to Paris to attend the Paris Peace Conference at Versailles.

When the United States entered World War I in April 1917, the Arkansas was attached to Battleship Division 7 and was patrolling the York River in Virginia where it entered the Atlantic. For the first few months of the war, the ship did patrol duty along the East Coast and trained gun crews to serve on armed merchant marine ships that were transporting men and arms to Europe. The postcard of the ship, framed in the stars and stripes, exhibited the patriotic message of the navy.

Seaman William A. Herz mailed this postcard of his image from aboard the Arkansas in May of 1917, a month after the United States entered the war against Germany. Although the ship would sail into the battle zones, aside from dropping a depth charge off Scotland on a suspected enemy U-boat, the Arkansas would not see battle during the remaining months of the war. Seaman Herz penned on the postcard, "Well and still alive. Sorry that Ruth is mad at me, tell her I still love her."

U. S. Dreadnaught Battleship "Arkansas" under full steam

DREADNAUGHT
T I R E S

To Dealers : DREADNAUGHT TIRES are easy to sell. On account of their attractive appearance—the handsome red treads contrasted with the soft-toned ivory side-walls—they immediately engage the attention of the public. Honestly built of the best and costliest materials on the market, they stand up against the hardest usage and give that smooth, velvety feeling to the car while riding at all speeds. They are in every way worthy of the name—DREADNAUGHT.

5000 MILES GUARANTEED

DREADNAUGHT Red "Silent" *Vacuum* Tread is a positive anti-skid. The bar through the center of the cups—an exclusive Dreadnaught design—prevents clogging, saves wear on the cups and tread, and minimizes that disagreeable humming noise accompanying non-skid devices. DREADNAUGHT Red *Ribbed* Tread is the front wheel favorite on account of its easy steering qualities.

Use SUPER-DREADNAUGHT RED INNER TUBES in Dreadnaught Tires—they are thicker and stronger than ordinary tubes. Dealers find them excellent leaders for their accessories stocks.

DEALERS—*We have an exceptional proposition and assure excellent service and territorial protection with intensive co-operation from our organization. Write or wire, Department "E"*

Beautifully illustrated Booklet "The Evolution of the Battleship" by Henry McDonald Spencer, sent free on request.

CHARLES F. U. KELLY, Inc.
Sales Department
1834 Broadway, New York

Manufactured by
The Dreadnaught Tire & Rubber Co.
Baltimore, Maryland

When writing advertisers please mention Motor World—it identifies you

The USS Arkansas *was one of the better-known ships in the U.S. Navy before and even during World War I, getting press notice for its port calls, especially in New York. The fame led to being showcased in the July 1917 edition of* Motor World *magazine to promote the Dreadnaught [sic] brand of tires, for which 5,000 miles of use was guaranteed. Dreadnought, translated as "fear nothing," was the class of warships after which the* Arkansas *had been styled.*

By the time the Arkansas *headed for the European theater of war, one of its sailors was Gilbert F. Holcomb, who had enlisted in May 1917 at the age of twenty-five. Holcomb would serve through the war aboard the ship, rising to a rank of Pattern Maker 1st Class, working with the ship's carpenters. When he was honorably discharged in July 1919, Holcomb took home an album of photographs he had taken during his service. He would live a long, successful life as the father of six children and as a successful builder of shopping centers and other commercial work for over fifty years. He died in 1973 at the age of eighty. Courtesy of Michael Pocock of Maritime Quest.*

Gilbert Holcomb's camera captured life aboard the ship, and he would return home after the war with one of the best legacies from the storied history of the USS Arkansas. The image captured here was of the ship's sailors, under the supervision of a U.S. Marine, performing machine gun drills on the deck. Courtesy of Michael Pocock of Maritime Quest.

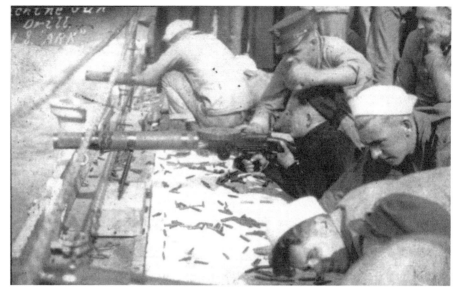

Some of Holcomb's photos captured views seldom photographed but that were carried in the memories of those who served aboard the ship all the same. The lens looked over the twelve-inch guns into the wake left behind the 27,000-ton Arkansas. Courtesy of Michael Pocock of Maritime Quest.

Group shots aboard the deck were popular and put Holcomb's camera in demand. Shown here, Gilbert Holcomb is the third from the left in the first row, next to the life ring in which sits one of the ship's mascot dogs. Courtesy Michael Pocock of Maritime Quest.

Sports were popular in the navy and served as an outlet for sailors often long at sea or confined to bases far from home. Gilbert Holcomb's camera captured a lot of the sporting activity aboard the Arkansas *during World War I. A boxing ring was set up often on the ship, sometimes to host a challenger from another ship, and a match always drew a crowd.* Courtesy of Michael Pocock of Maritime Quest.

Although less popular than boxing, wrestling matches were also popular with Arkansas sailors not tied to their posts. Some of the sailors watched the match shown here from atop the barrels of the ship's twelve-inch guns. Courtesy of Michael Pocock of Maritime Quest.

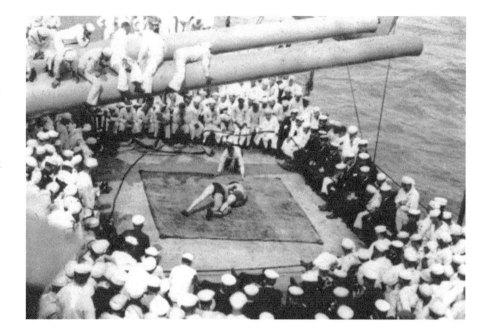

Seaman Holcomb photographed the crew at work, not just at play, and there was plenty of work to do in the massive ship housing more than 1,000 men. A battleship of the era was in many ways a self-contained city, with all manner of craftsmen on board such as carpenters, electricians, painters, cooks, and medical personnel, as well as those taking care of the weapons. Courtesy Michael Pocock of Maritime Quest.

While not losing a man to enemy fire during World War I, the Arkansas was not without losses among its crew from illness and accidents. Seaman A. H. Gloeckle was working on reloading one of the fifty-foot steam-powered picket boats (shown here) that the warship carried for shore landings where dockage was not possible. While the smaller vessel was being lifted back onto the Arkansas, one of the slings supporting it broke, and the picket boat struck Gloeckle in the head, killing him.

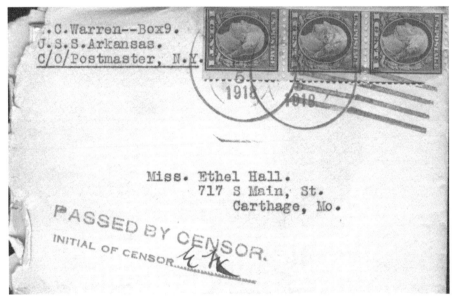

Serving aboard the Arkansas in European waters during World War I was Z. C. Warren, who wrote many letters to Miss Ethel Hall of Carthage, Missouri. As evidenced by the envelope in the photograph, all the letters were censored—and read before mailing by assigned navy inspectors. Seaman Warren was careful to not ever reveal the location of the ship in his letters, which would have failed the censor inspection if he had, and would never have been seen by Miss Hall.

The guns, both at sea and on land, would fall silent on November 11, 1918, with the armistice to end the so-called War to End All Wars. World War I was over and the crew of the USS Arkansas had a lot to celebrate for Christmas. One of the sailors, J. H. Lavender, mailed the Christmas card shown here, which had been published recognizing the ship's service in the conflict.

This picture was taken by a World War I sailor aboard the Arkansas, with this penciled in the margin of his album: "the only flag that has ever flown above Old Glory" (the Christian flag on a day of worship).

72002 U. S. S. ARKANSAS AND NEW YORK SKYLINE

The USS Arkansas was present off the coast of Scotland on November 21, 1918, when, as required by the Armistice, Germany surrendered its navy, some seventy-five warships and 20,000 crew members. The British would later sink the ships, some 400,000 tons of vessels, in the largest single day sinking in history. The Arkansas finally sailed for New York, arriving under the Brooklyn Bridge to throngs of grateful Americans giving tribute.

For more than two
decades following the
end of World War I,
the *USS* Arkansas
busied herself with
matters of protocol,
receiving ambassadors,
participating in
centennials, and, in
general, serving as a
goodwill ambassador
to the world.

Chapter Five

Between the Wars

In the months after the war, the officers of the *Arkansas* got a major upgrade to their dining experience. A silver service set valued at $10,000 was presented by the State of Arkansas to its namesake battleship in April 1919. The silver service, presented to the ship's officers by Little Rock artist Daisy Dalony on behalf of Governor Charles Brough, would be used often in the years between the wars. In July 1919, the *Arkansas* was assigned to the U.S. Pacific Fleet. For more than two decades following the end of World War I, the USS *Arkansas* busied herself with matters of protocol, receiving ambassadors, participating in centennials, and, in general, serving as a goodwill ambassador to the world.[1]

A major means of communication on the *Arkansas* throughout her more than three decades of service was the ship's newspaper, the *Arklight*. Initially issued monthly, later varying between bi-weekly and weekly, the paper reflected happenings aboard, carried news, and relayed messages from the ship's captain.

Religious services were a prominent part of life aboard the *Arkansas* during the 1920s, and these were promoted in the newspaper. The March 26, 1921, edition of the *Arklight* announced Easter services while the ship was anchored in New York City: "The greatest day in the Church Calendar is that of Easter Sunday. At this time we celebrate the Resurrection of our Lord and Savior Jesus Christ. It is a time of Hope, of the taking on of New Life. What does this religious event mean to you? Attend Church on the quarter deck tomorrow morning at 9:30. Holy Communion will be observed at the close of the service. The Catholic Church party will go to *New York* [the sister battleship moored nearby]."

The degree to which the *Arkansas* was a self-contained city of commerce and craftsmanship was evident in a March 1921 piece in the

Arklight titled "Patronize Your Home Industries," which stated, "The cobbler shop has recently been fitted with a thousand dollar outfit of up-to-date shoe repairing machinery. One officer who recently had a pair of half soles sewed on praises the work of the cobbler shop very highly. It is a lot cheaper than ashore and you help swell the Ship's Service Fund by having your work done onboard."

The *Arklight* published a page of jokes submitted weekly by the crew, many not politically correct in today's world, though some would bring a laugh decades later. This joke appeared in the November 1920 edition:

> **Father:** I understand you were severely punished by the teacher today.
> **Son:** Yes, and it was all your fault.
> **Father:** How's that?
> **Son:** Well, yesterday I asked you what a million was, and you said, "A heluvalot," and that wasn't the answer at all.

A South American voyage highlighted the *Arkansas*'s 1921 activities. For a number of years, she participated in U.S. Naval Academy midshipman summer practice cruises to European waters. On her 1923 midshipman cruise, she called at Copenhagen, Denmark, where she was visited by that nation's king. On a 1925 midshipman cruise to the western coast of the United States, she arrived at Santa Barbara, California, in the aftermath of an earthquake. The *Arkansas*, along with the *McCawley* and the *Eagle*, landed a patrol of bluejackets with orders to police the city and establish a radio station for the transmission of messages.

Upon completion of her 1925 midshipmen cruise, the *Arkansas* entered the Philadelphia Naval Yard for extensive modernization. Her aging coal-burning boilers were replaced with new oil-powered ones. Additional deck armor was installed, a single smokestack was substituted for the original pair, and the after cage mast was replaced by a low tripod. Under the command of Captain Amon Bronson Jr., the revitalized battleship left the Naval Yard in November 1926 for a shakedown cruise along the eastern seaboard and to Cuban waters before returning to Philadelphia to undergo acceptance trials.[2]

Reporting for duty with the fleet, the *Arkansas* was present on September 5, 1927, at ceremonies unveiling a memorial tablet honoring the French soldiers who died during the campaign at Yorktown, Virginia, in 1781. Following a midshipman practice cruise along the East Coast, the vessel operated near the Panama Canal Zone and in Caribbean waters. In May 1929, she docked at the New York Naval Yard for repairs

On a 1925 midshipman cruise to the western coast of the United States, she arrived at Santa Barbara, California, in the aftermath of an earthquake. The Arkansas, *along with the* McCawley *and the* Eagle, *landed a patrol of bluejackets with orders to police the city and establish a radio station for the transmission of messages.*

The cover page of the May 12, 1934, edition of the Arklight *urged the sailors to remember Mother's Day. "Everyman who has a mother living should write to her on Mother's Day."*

before embarking on a midshipman cruise to the Mediterranean and English waters. The warship closed out the year on patrol with the Scouting Fleet off the East Coast.

Throughout the 1930s, the USS *Arkansas* continued to engage in numerous tests and maneuvers, anchoring in exotic ports of call and hosting a parade of dignitaries. In 1930, she visited Cherbourg, France; Kiel, Germany; Oslo, Norway, and Edinburgh, Scotland. The following year, she docked at Copenhagen; Greenock, Scotland; and Cadiz, Spain, as well as Gibraltar. In October 1931, following a visit to Halifax, Nova Scotia, Canada, the *Arkansas* participated in the sesquicentennial celebration of the Battle of Yorktown, transporting President Herbert Hoover and his entourage to the exposition. Three days later, she transported the presidential party back to Annapolis, Maryland.

The battleship sailed in January 1932, calling at New Orleans, Louisiana, to take part in that city's colorful Mardi Gras celebration. She proceeded through the Panama Canal for a tour of Pacific duty. The *Arkansas* was designated as the flagship of the Pacific Fleet's Training Squadron in 1934.[3]

The March 24, 1934, edition of the *Arklight* carried news of coming port calls but also of re-enlistments of men on board, along with those who had been awarded good conduct medals. One of those awarded such a medal was Joe Dimes Jr., who had enlisted at Little Rock in 1928, listing his home address as a rural route in Bonanza, Arkansas, located in Sebastian County. The same edition's humor page also carried this joke:

> **Pastor:** This morning I will have for my topic "The Great Flood of Genesis."
> **Prominent member of congregation (rising):** I've got an engagement to play golf so I can't stay, but I'll head the subscription list with $1,000 to relieve the suffering Genesians.

The cover page of the May 12, 1934, edition of the *Arklight* urged the sailors to remember Mother's Day. "Every man who has a mother living should write to her on Mother's Day."

In the summer of 1934, according to the *Arklight*, the ship conducted a midshipman practice cruise to Plymouth, England; Nice, France; Naples, Italy; and Gibraltar. Returning to Annapolis in August, she was ordered to Newport, Rhode Island, where her crew manned the rail as President Franklin D. Roosevelt sailed past on the yacht *Nourmahal*. The *Arkansas* took part in Newport's annual International Yacht Race, defeating the cutter from the British light cruiser HMS *Dragon* for the Battenberg Cup and the City of Newport Cup. It was a carefree time for the aging battleship and her crew, with no concern of war clouds gathering around the globe.

For the next three years, with the exception of midshipman summer practice cruises to Europe, the *Arkansas*'s duties with the Naval Training Squadron largely confined her to the eastern seaboard. The outbreak of war in Europe in September 1939 found the *Arkansas* at Hampton Roads, Virginia, preparing for another Naval Reserve cruise. She soon got under way, transporting seaplane moorings and aviation equipment from the Norfolk Naval Air Station to Narragansett Bay, Rhode Island, where a new seaplane base was being established.

A new mission for the warship came in September 1939 with the assignment of the *Arkansas* to serve as part of the American Neutrality Patrol, only eight days after the outbreak of fighting in Europe. The United States was officially neutral at that point in facing the rapidly rising threat from Hitler in Europe, but it was transparent in its sympathies for the Allied cause. The *Arkansas*, along with the slightly younger battleships *New York* and *Texas*, patrolled for three-week stretches along the edge of the European war zone in the Atlantic. The task was to take part in observation and reconnaissance of Axis warships. With the exception of an unsuccessful U-boat attack against the *Texas*, the patrols were without incident.

The *Arkansas*, accompanied by the *Texas* and the *New York*, departed Norfolk in January 1940 for fleet exercises at Guantanamo Bay, Cuba. Following further training activities, the ship made her last midshipman summer practice cruise, sailing to Panama and Venezuela. Before the close of the year, the *Arkansas* would undertake Naval Reserve training cruises to Guantanamo Bay, the Panama Canal Zone, and Chesapeake Bay. It now seemed all but inevitable that the United States would eventually be drawn into the conflict on the side of England, France, and Russia against Germany and Italy. In Asia, the armed forces of Japan were also on the march, bent on establishing the vast empire that its warlords deemed appropriate for a modern industrial giant. Most Americans, however, did not view Japan as a serious threat. To most Americans, Adolf Hitler was the enemy.

The *Arkansas*'s serving in any coming war was not considered likely. The ship was nearing her thirtieth birthday, one of the oldest ships left in the navy, and her crew could not imagine the old ship ever seeing a war zone again. New battleships with greater speed and more armaments were the vanguard of any modern navy, relegating ships like the *Arkansas* mostly to training missions along the eastern seaboard of the United States. The Arky's age was beginning to show, and the navy's plan was

The Arkansas*'s serving in any coming war was not considered likely. The ship was nearing her thirtieth birthday, one of the oldest ships left in the navy, and her crew could not imagine the old ship ever seeing a war zone again.*

After the historic meeting, the twenty-nine-year-old battleship USS Arkansas was ordered to Casco Bay, Maine, to await a summons to the retirement list, decommissioning, and, in all likelihood, a final voyage to the scrapyard. Fate, however, had other plans for the aging warrior.

to replace the ship in 1941, when the *North Carolina* was scheduled to be completed. The new ship would have sixteen-inch guns versus the twelve-inch guns on the *Arkansas*. The *Arkansas* would then be decommissioned and scrapped—of that there seemed little doubt.[4]

With the United States edging toward war in the Atlantic, President Franklin Roosevelt decided in late June 1941 to establish an outer bulwark in Iceland. Commanded by Captain Carleton F. Bryant, the *Arkansas*, along with the *New York* and the light cruiser *Brooklyn*, escorted the first contingent of American troops to Reykjavik, Iceland. With the United States still officially on the sidelines of the expanding world conflict, the *Arkansas* proceeded to relieve British forces that had occupied the island a year earlier but that were needed back in Europe. The British had first occupied the often frigid island after the Germans had moved into Denmark, knowing they next had set their sights on Iceland for a radar station. The United States, despite its official neutral status, did not want to see the Germans establish a foothold in Iceland, given its proximity to the shipping lanes of the North Atlantic.

Following her mission to Iceland, the *Arkansas* sailed to Newfoundland. She was present when the Atlantic Charter Conference took place on board the USS *Augusta* between American president Franklin Roosevelt and British prime minister Winston Churchill. During the conference, the *Arkansas* provided accommodations for Under Secretary of State Summer Welles and presidential advisor W. Averell Harriman.[5]

After the historic meeting, the twenty-nine-year-old battleship USS *Arkansas* was ordered to Casco Bay, Maine, to await a summons to the retirement list, decommissioning, and, in all likelihood, a final voyage to the scrapyard. Fate, however, had other plans for the aging warrior.

After a shakedown inspection and repair at the Norfolk, Virginia, shipyards, the Arkansas was assigned to the Pacific Fleet, necessitating passage through the Panama Canal. Shown here, the ship is passing through the Culbera Cut, which had been one of the most difficult parts of building the canal a few years earlier.

The Arkansas would make a number of passages through the Panama Canal over its more than three decades of service, both in times of war and in training missions. The photo here shows how the huge warship barely fit in the narrow lock, with much of its crew on deck to witness the powerful dockside track-mounted engines guiding the ship, with taut cables on both sides, through the locks, keeping it from touching the concrete walls.

The Arkansas *shared passage through the Panama Canal locks with the USS Texas en route to the Pacific. The two ships, both of which had been commissioned in 1912, would pass each other in a number of places over the years. The ships had both been at the Veracruz invasion, and would both later support the Normandy invasion in World War II. Today, the Texas is a floating museum anchored at San Jacinto, Texas. Official U.S. Navy photo.*

Photo # NH 57682 USS Arkansas & USS Texas in Gatun Locks, Panama Canal, 25 July 1919

The USS Arkansas's *complement of officers wore their dress white uniforms for a top-deck view of the passage through the Panama Canal around 1920.*

U.S.S. Arkansas from Airplane

ON DECK "ARKANSAS"

The Arkansas *visited San Francisco in 1919, photographed here from a plane off the shore. The ship would take on board Navy Secretary Josephus Daniels and his wife for a continued passage up the Pacific Coast to Puget Sound near Seattle. Secretary Daniels had been in charge of the navy for nearly a decade, having overseen it during World War I. It was by his orders in 1914 that prohibition of alcohol was made the law for the navy. He also issued the orders to ban prostitution within five miles of all U.S. Navy bases. In Seattle, the ship would be reviewed by President Woodrow Wilson, who had last seen her off the coast of Europe at the end of World War I the previous year.*

When docked during peacetime, as in Seattle, the ship drew spectators and even visitors on board during certain hours to allow the public a close-up look at life on the deck of an American warship. The fashionably dressed women strolling the deck of a ship less than a year removed from a war zone elicited conversations we can only imagine almost a century later.

Training sailors and Coast Guard men was an important role for the Arkansas in the decades between world wars. A key part of that, for which the ship was renowned, was the accuracy with which it could fire its battery of guns. The training both day and at night (shown here) simulated a variety of targets and conditions. This photo—taken off the deck of the Arkansas—shows a floating target that had been towed into place. Penciled on the back of the photo is "evidence of the Arkansas Efficiency."

This photo shows the view the sailors operating the Arkansas's twelve-inch guns would have had of their handiwork.

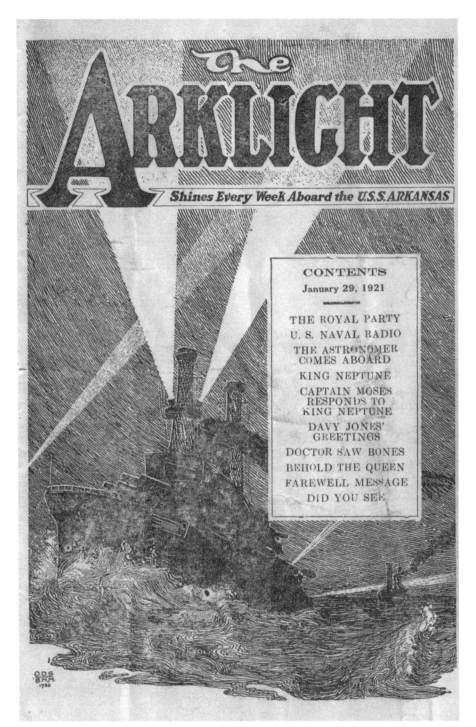

THE
ARKLIGHT

Shines Every Week Aboard the U.S.S. ARKANSAS

CONTENTS
January 29, 1921

THE ROYAL PARTY
U.S. NAVAL RADIO
THE ASTRONOMER
COMES ABOARD
KING NEPTUNE
CAPTAIN MOSES
RESPONDS TO
KING NEPTUNE
DAVY JONES'
GREETINGS
DOCTOR SAW BONES
BEHOLD THE QUEEN
FAREWELL MESSAGE
DID YOU SEE

The ship's onboard newspaper, the Arklight, often noted with pride the winning scores the ship earned in competing with other vessels in the accuracy of its gun crews. The ship's newspaper started publishing during World War I, first monthly but later weekly. The ship's commanders encouraged the sailors to mail the publication home to friends and family. Today, copies still turn up around the world.

The commanding officer and his senior staff saw a major improvement in their dining experience in April 1919 with the presentation of a set of silver valued around $10,000. Today, parts of the silver service are on loan to both the Arkansas Governor's Mansion and the MacArthur Museum of Arkansas Military History in Little Rock.

With the war over and the Arkansas returned to training missions, the ship's crew turned a lot of its spare time and competitive spirit toward sports. The 1919–20 ship's baseball team posed here ashore, having played teams from other ships at various bases and ports of call.

One of the ship's rowing teams is pictured here, showing off a large trophy on the deck.

The 1919–20 ship's basketball team posed on the deck of the warship.

TOP 'O THE HEAP
ARKANSAS
IN GUNNERY ATHLETICS N' EVERYTHING
PACIFIC   ATLANTIC
HENDOAK

Even Uncle Sam was proud of the winning ways of the USS Arkansas teams, proclaiming the athletic crews "Top 'o the Heap" in everything for both the Atlantic and the Pacific. The cartoon was likely drawn by a crewman of the Arkansas for publication in the Arklight.

In the 1920s, the USS Arkansas *published its own small sports magazine, 5 Minutes of Ark. Stories in the June 20, 1925, edition included the ship's basketball team playing in the Panama Canal Zone against the Balboa High School team, swim meets, and "Navy Sluggers Getting Underway," in which a baseball game was won 6–0.*

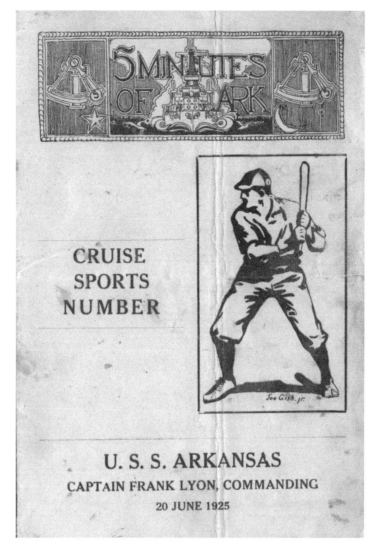

Captain Ridley McLean *commanded the ship from 1922 to 1924. An 1894 Naval Academy graduate, Captain McLean had won the Navy Cross during World War I. He was credited with pioneering the use of the shortwave radio for the navy, going on to be promoted to rear admiral. Commanding the USS Nevada, he died aboard the ship of a heart attack in 1933. Some fifty warships assembled for his funeral service, held on the deck of the ship. He is buried at Arlington National Cemetery.*

During the peaceful 1920s, in her various training missions, the Arkansas docked in Havana, Cuba, and at the U.S. naval base at Guantanamo Bay. The United States had won Cuba in the Spanish-American War in 1898 but had given the island nation self-rule in 1909. The photo here, with the old Spanish fort in the background, was taken around 1927.

Shore leave was much anticipated by the crew when the Arkansas docked in Cuba. A "recreation party" was captured on a postcard in the 1920s, the crew having used one of the ship's launches to come ashore.

69

Perhaps some of the recreation related to the young ladies of Havana, shown here in a postcard a sailor on the ship put into a scrapbook. The postcard states, "The Beautiful Havana Belles are infatuated with the Handsome Young American Sailor."

The Beautiful Havana Belles are infatuated with the Handsome Young American Sailor

R. B. Sawmiller entered the navy in 1937. While serving aboard the Arkansas, he compiled a photo album that included a photo of him and companions posing with some local liquor on the Cuban docks. Which sailor is Sawmiller is not known. Of note is the black sailor in the back row of the group.

In contrast to the sometimes rowdy seamen on shore leave were the officers in dress uniform attending functions in the finer buildings of Havana. The medal-adorned captain did not record his name on the photo.

Whether docked in port or steaming across the ocean, the massive USS Arkansas required constant maintenance. One of the more unpopular jobs was cleaning the wooden deck. This photo was taken during the annual cruise for midshipmen in July 1930.

In January 1929, the Arkansas *sailed down the East River, passing the New York City skyline, bound for Hampton Roads, Virginia. The ship was scheduled to help greet the president-elect, Herbert Hoover, at a ceremony in Virginia. After that, she sailed south for winter maneuvers in warmer climates.*

In November 1930, the Arkansas *was photographed upon arrival in New York. A note with the photograph reads, "The bridge of sighs,— but they're sighs of joy! You can almost hear the expressions of delight as the USS Arkansas, her men drawn up at attention on deck, glides majestically under the Brooklyn Bridge on her way to her berth in the Brooklyn Navy Yard. The TARS [the sailors] will have a chance to enjoy their Thanksgiving holidays around festive boards heaped high with the traditional feast." The Empire State building, only months away from its official opening, is visible in the center of the skyline.*

The Arkansas was docked off California's Catalina Island in 1933. The occasion provided a photo-op for Mac, Juanita, and Bill Moore. The uniformed youngsters were the grandchildren of the late Admiral William Moffett, who had once commanded the ship. Their father, E. McFarlane Moore, had also served aboard the ship until 1926, and he was able to take them aboard the day this photo was taken.

When upon the open sea, some of the sailors and marines took a chance to show off their marksmanship, trying to hit clay skeet pigeons fired from a launcher on the deck. In the background of this 1930 photo is an observation plane that could be launched by catapult from the deck.

In October 1931, Marshal Henre Petain of France was photographed at Yorktown, Virginia, boarding the Arkansas, saluting the crew as he came onto the deck. The French official had come to greet President Herbert Hoover. Both would attend the 150th anniversary of British general Cornwallis's surrender to George Washington. It was in part the aid of the French that had helped the Americans defeat the British.

While the ship was docked in U.S. ports, civilian visitors in the years between the world wars were afforded surprising access when touring the Arkansas. A young woman is shown here getting a gun-crew's-eye view down the sights of one of the ship's five-inch guns.

Though apparently never deployed during combat, the Arkansas was equipped and armed with two torpedo tubes mounted near the water line on the side of the ship. During a training exercise in the 1930s, an aerial photograph captured the firing of a torpedo at a target, with the wake of the torpedo visible in a clear, straight line.

STATEHOOD
DAY
ARKANSAS
ADMITTED
TO THE UNION
JUNE 15, 1836

U.S.S. ARKANSAS. JUN 15 9 A.M. LONG C

Mr. W. J. Kirby,
Dermott, Arkansas

While the ship was anchored in Long Beach, California, someone on the Arkansas sent a letter to Dermott, Arkansas, in recognition of the 100th anniversary of Arkansas statehood.

The Arkansas *paid a visit to the port in Kiel, Germany, in the summer of 1936. The German sailors on their warship, the SMS Schleswig-Holstein, assembled to salute their American visitors, who at the same time lined the deck of the* Arkansas *at anchor in the harbor. The Schleswig had been commissioned in 1905. It would have the distinction of firing the first shots of World War II, firing on a Polish naval base in September 1939. The German warship was sunk by British bombers in 1944.*

The officers of the Arkansas *welcomed their fellow German navy officers from the* Schleswig *aboard and posed for a photo in their dress uniforms. Little could the smiling men have known that within fewer than six years, they would be at war with one another.*

During her decades of service, the USS Arkansas *maintained close ties to the U.S. Marine Corps, which depended on the ship for transport and training exercises. Photographed here in California in the late 1930s, a detachment of marines came on board for transport, carrying their rifles and gear. Visible above their heads are some of the observation float planes the* Arkansas *carried.*

Scout-observation planes were attached to battleships like the Arkansas *and were designed to be hurled off the ships by powerful catapults. One of the planes, which were sometimes called "seagulls" by the sailors, had just been launched from the* Arkansas; *one of the ship's lifeboats can be seen below. The plane, a Curtiss SOC-2 seaplane, was a two-seater, with a thirty-five-foot wingspan. When fully loaded, each weighed just over 5,000 pounds.*

The manner in which the scout-observation planes were carried is illustrated by this photo showing two of the planes suspended over the twelve-inch guns of the Arkansas in the summer of 1936. The navy purchased 250 of the planes between 1935 and 1937. Powered by a 550 H.P. Pratt and Whitney engine, the planes claimed a top speed of 165 mph, with a range of 900 miles. They could carry two 30-caliber machine guns and several small bombs.

These marines were photographed on what seems to have been a cold day, carrying their bedding and ducking their heads beneath the twelve-inch guns of the Arkansas. The sailor at the left was directing the marines below deck to their temporary quarters.

Members of the Arkansas crew had a short leave to London in July 1937 during a training cruise. The sailors here were photographed in Trafalgar Square, not far from a statue of Lord Nelson, referred to by the British photographer as "the greatest sailor of all time."

HOME FROM
THE SEA
"You'll have to
ke her back, son.
anged if I'll have
dottern-law livin'
t th' horse
ugh!"

Seaman R. B. Sawmiller clipped a lot of navy-related cartoons, adding them to his scrapbook during his service on the Arkansas. One of these, titled "Home from the Sea," read: "You'll have to take her back, son. Danged if I'll have a dottern-law livin' in th' horse trough!"

Mermaids were on the mind of an Arkansas sailor docked in France in 1934 when he added some art work to an envelope mailed to Connecticut.

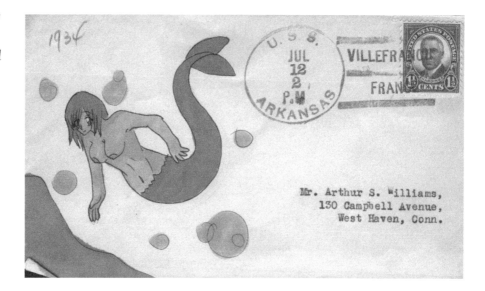

Perhaps it reminded Seaman Sawmiller of one of his experiences, but he glued in his scrapbook a picture of a young woman seeing off a sailor who happened to spy a photo in her purse of an army man.

"Modern Salts spinning a tale" was the caption given a photo of relaxing Arkansas sailors in 1940. Such photos would have played a role in recruiting young men to join the navy and see the world.

One of the last photos in Sawmiller's scrapbook was this one, perhaps of himself, though it is not so labeled. The young sailor was posed atop the barrel of one of the Arkansas's twelve-inch guns, barrels as long as a railroad boxcar.

Not long before Sawmiller's scrapbook and four-year enlistment ended, in July 1941, he received a letter denying him the Good Conduct Medal. Why would he have kept such a seemingly negative correspondence? The answer likely lies with the name at the bottom: C. W. Nimitz, then chief of the Navy Department's Bureau of Navigation. Better known later in the midst of World War II as Fleet Admiral Chester Nimitz, he became one of the best-known figures in twentieth-century naval history. Nimitz commanded all the U.S. Navy Pacific operations during World War II.

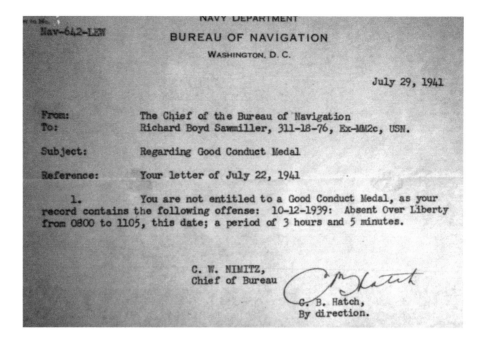

Chapter Six

D-Day Heroism

As the Allied invasions of North Africa got under way in 1943, the ship found herself supporting troops landing in such exotic ports as Casablanca, all the while taking evasive measures from German submarines picked up on radar.

The Japanese attack on Pearl Harbor on Sunday, December 7, 1941, found the USS *Arkansas* at anchor in Casco Bay, Maine. Within a week of the U.S. declaration of war, plans for decommissioning and scrapping the thirty-year-old ship were dropped and the old battleship was stripped down to lighten her for faster travel. The loss of much of the U.S. Pacific Fleet meant that every available ship was going to be needed in what was now a worldwide conflict. The removal of trophies won in years of fleet competition in a variety of target and sports competitions alone accounted for a decrease in weight of hundreds of pounds. Before Christmas 1941, the *Arkansas* was on patrol off the coast of Iceland.

The *Arkansas*, after major renovations at the shipyards of Norfolk, Virginia, in the spring of 1942, would spend the first year or so of the war escorting convoys of supply ships and troops across the North Atlantic: "Bombs, shells, planes, tanks, guns, gasoline and U.S. troops were hauled through sub-infested, fog-shrouded North Atlantic to points in England, Scotland and Ireland."[1] To the *Arkansas* went the job of shepherding the jammed troop transports and cargo carriers.

Captain Fredrick C. Richards assumed command of the USS *Arkansas* on May 5, 1943. Three weeks later, the ship headed to Chesapeake Bay, where she helped train Naval Academy midshipmen until returning to convoy escort duty in October.

As the Allied invasions of North Africa got under way in 1943, the ship found herself supporting troops landing in such exotic ports as Casablanca, all the while taking evasive measures from German submarines picked up on radar. Until the spring of 1944, the *Arkansas*'s work was confined to "routine" escorts of troop transport and convoy ships. The captain and the crew were proud of the fact that during numerous

The ship was sent to serve off the coast of Ireland to train for a new challenge, one she had not faced in her thirty-year existence: She was to shell shorelines and dug-in enemy troops to assist an Allied landing. The history of D-Day, the most massive landing in military history, would number among its heroes the crew of the USS Arkansas.

Atlantic crossings, not a single Allied ship under the protection of the *Arkansas*'s guns was lost or damaged by the enemy.

On April 18, 1944, the word went out to the crew of the *Arkansas* that her convoy and troop transport duties were over and that she was being called for much heavier duty. "USS *Arkansas* was ready for the more militant role of which a militant capital ship was deserving."[2]

The ship was sent to serve off the coast of Ireland to train for a new challenge, one she had not faced in her thirty-year existence: She was to shell shorelines and dug-in enemy troops to assist an Allied landing. The history of D-Day, the most massive landing in military history, would number among its heroes the crew of the USS *Arkansas*.

Though the crew did not know the details of the coming invasion or the location, those aboard the *Arkansas* knew a major battle was drawing nigh. On May 30, 1944, a young sailor, David Roberts, penned in his journal: "Captain Richards [F. G. Richards, *Arkansas* commander] made a broadcast over the public address system. He has never before addressed his crew like he did then. His solemn voice spoke words with knowledge and he expressed his opinions of the crew & task. A few quotations from his speech included, 'We are now on our way to participate in the biggest naval and military operation of all time. You are a good fighting and good shooting crew. It's going to be plenty tough at all times but I believe you are ready. You've been trained by months of sea duty and the many drills and maneuvers we have been having. It's up to you fellows.'"

An eighteen-year-old Gunners Mate 3rd Class, Anthony Arthur Sirco, was aboard the *Arkansas* as it prepared to participate in the D-Day invasion. Sirco had grown up in the Bronx, the son of a Polish immigrant mother and a Ukrainian immigrant father. Young Sirco had joined the U.S. Navy at the age of seventeen in July 1943, and a month later, found himself assigned to the *Arkansas*. The young man would keep a handwritten journal throughout his service in both the European and Pacific theaters of World War II.

Two entries are related here:

May 31, 1944, as of 0001 (12:01 a.m.) the ship was officially sealed. That is no person shall have contact with anyone outside of the ship. Also today we received gas masks just in case the Germans try to use gas.

June 1, 1944, At 1300 (1:00 p.m.) the commanding officer addressed the crew. At 1415 (2:15 p.m.) giving out facts of the invasion. At 1415 we found out we were to bombard Northern France covering up the invading First Army. With us (Arkansas) will be two French cruisers Montcalm and [Georges Leygues], 2 British Destroyers, 2 American destroyers. Also there will be 4,000 ships in our invasion force alone. We received flash proof gloves and face masks.

Gunners Mate Sirco was assigned to the ship's Fifth Division, with his duties on the big twelve-inch guns. Sirco picked up again on June 2:

> Today we are stowing all burnable material and any other loose gear. We also received more D-Day information. For eight hours before the invasion 4,500 planes will be bombing France. When they have exhausted their bombs and fuel, 4,500 other planes will relieve them and so forth. They will be relieving each other every 45 minutes so that there will be a continuous line of planes as described in this figure.

The young sailor drew in his notes a circular diagram showing a continuous loop of bombers between France and bases in England that were constantly refueling and rearming:

> There will be hundreds of transport planes carrying paratroopers. The transports will fly in single file as the paratroopers leap.

Sirco picked up his journal pen again at 2 a.m. on June 3:

> We (Arkansas) got underway presumably going to invasion point No. France.

The *Nevada*, *Texas*, *Montcalm*, and *Georges Leygues* were sailing in the formation through the pitch-dark English Channel. The enormity of the invasion force was reflected in Sirco's next entry at 3:45 in the afternoon of June 3:

> We met some ships, the number being so great it was impossible to count them. At 8:15 PM we met another 59 ships. These ships were empty, were to be used as decoys.

Richard Kelly was serving his country aboard the *Arkansas* as it trained off Ireland, and the entire crew knew something major was in its near future. Kelly would write the following after the fact:

> We left Bangor (County Antrim, Ireland) on 3 June. The invasion was to be on the morning of the 6th, as you probably know. The ship was sealed. No one could go ashore after, oh, I'd say about 31 May. They sealed the ship. Were all anchored off Bangor, the whole invasion fleet. Only the high-ranking officers that had business were permitted to shore for any reason. We were shown detailed maps and everything off Omaha beachhead where we would be based. I would say we were shown the relief maps 2 June.[3]

"Today we are stowing all burnable material and any other loose gear. We also received more D-Day information. For eight hours before the invasion 4,500 planes will be bombing France. When they have exhausted their bombs and fuel, 4,500 other planes will relieve them and so forth."

When World War II began, the USS Arkansas was docked at Casco Bay, Maine. The ship had been in service for twenty-nine years and was awaiting retirement and scrapping. The "Arky," as many of her crew had coined her, was old and had become obsolete in an era of newer, more modern warships. The loss of much of the Pacific Fleet at Pearl Harbor, however, changed a lot of plans for the Navy, and for the Arkansas. The old lady still had history to make.

The Arkansas spent part of the summer of 1942 in the Norfolk, Virginia, Naval Yard undergoing extensive renovations to prepare the thirty-year-old ship to fight in World War II, a much different war than World War I. The ship that was scheduled for the scrap yard a few months earlier was now being retrofitted to sail into a world at war.

Seaman Dave Roberts, a teenager from Tennessee, was keeping a personal journal aboard the *Arkansas* as D-Day approached. He wrote down the pep talk the collective task force of ships was given on June 3, 1944, by their commander, Rear Admiral Bryant:

What a pleasure it is to have together the battleships of Battleship Division Five. We are on an important and dangerous mission. Heads up, tails over the dashboard. If the going gets tough close up and slug it out.

Seaman David Roberts, in his personal journal, continued updating daily the experiences of preparing for D-Day:

June 4, 1944, D Day delayed 24 hours. Still cruising.
June 5, 1944, Task Force has been cruising around between Plymouth and Lands End awaiting for weather to clear. Today the fog lifted and we are proceeding to the Isle of Wight at present time for a rendezvous at sea. We will proceed on to France this night and attack at dawn. We have to go about 100 miles to reach the coast of France. Tonight we will go through the German mine fields. There are around 65 miles of these fields.

Anthony Sirco was also journaling in the early dawn of June 4, 1944:

Word was passed that D-Day would be delayed for 24 hours. Now we are just cruising around waiting for things to pop. It was too misty for the planes to bomb France.

At 9:00 a.m., Sirco recorded a jolting occurrence:

Destroyer *Jefferson* dropped 3 depth charges just 2,000 yards off our starboard bow. That sure shook hell out of us.

He next recorded news in the evening from a nearby ship:

USS *Texas* had a sea burial for a man who suddenly died.

The next day, June 5, Gunners Mate Sirco opened his notes at 8:23 a.m.:

Our force headed towards France. We received news that Rome had fallen.

"We will proceed on to France this night and attack at dawn. We have to go about 100 miles to reach the coast of France. Tonight we will go through the German mine fields. There are around 65 miles of these fields."

Three decades earlier, in 1914, the Arkansas had landed large numbers of men at Veracruz, Mexico. Still, nothing had been seen before on the scale that would be the D-Day invasion on the Normandy coast of France.

By 10:38 a.m. he had penciled:

We went to battle stations in preparation for shelling the coast of France about 10 hours later. 6:22 pm, the first marker was dropped, showing the way in. Just in case we have to leave in a hurry we can get out the mined area without mishap.
8:17 PM we met a large group of troopships.
11:42 we are 35 miles from the French coast. Anti-aircraft fire can be seen on the coast.
1417 hours we passed two groups of L.S.T.s [landingcraft], 37 in all. The soldiers on them were packed like sardines.

Amphibious landings had been worked on by the navy for years. However, shore bombardment had been attempted only once, in 1943 on the island of Tarawa in the South Pacific, with limited success. Three decades earlier, in 1914, the *Arkansas* had landed large numbers of men at Veracruz, Mexico. Still, nothing had been seen before on the scale that would be the D-Day invasion on the Normandy coast of France. The Germans had been fortifying the cliffs and beaches for months, knowing that an Allied attempt to retake the Continent was coming. Under Adolf Hitler's orders, they were determined to hurl the Allies back into the sea.

The Allies, led by General Dwight D. Eisenhower, knew that a massive amount of naval firepower would be essential in softening up the Germans' Normandy defenses, from concrete-reinforced pillboxes shielding all manner of guns to the tidal-edge barriers intended to hamper landingcraft. The guns of the *Arkansas*, *Texas*, and *Nevada*—all World War I–vintage ships—were going to be vital to the success of any landing.

The combination of tension and excitement present on the ship as it sailed to help liberate Europe was expressed in the pages of *U.S.S. Arkansas Pictorial Review*, published at the end of 1944 by the U.S. Navy. Though told in the first person, the text does not give a name of the sailor writing:

When we started into the channels leading toward the landing area, we were all keyed-up to a high pitch; and then, when D-day was post-poned for a day because of unfavorable seas and weather, we were left hanging high and dry in an emotional pitch, having steeled ourselves for what was to come. As the weather opened up and, once more, we began to move toward the landing area, gathering ships as we went; we became accustomed to the electric tension in the air. We were in a constant state of alertness those few hours previous to H-hour, for we were passing through heavily mined waters all the time. As H-hour drew nearer, there was a marked quietness about the ship, for it was still very dark, and every turn of the engines brought us nearer to, we knew not what. Over in the east, there was only the faintest hint of approaching dawn. At last, what had appeared to have been an unusually high horizon, and toward which I had been steadily training my binoculars, began to take on definite shapes and outlines, and I realized that it was not more water, but the coast of France—Normandy.[4]

In the pre-dawn darkness of June 6, 1944, the *Arkansas* took up her assigned position 4,000 yards off Omaha beach. While it was still dark, the signs of battle were already detected by the hundreds of sailors manning the old battleship. The air was filled with the sounds of aircraft zooming overhead, the explosions on the shore lighting up the night as they dropped bombs on the dug-in German positions. Surrounding the *Arkansas* were hundreds of smaller ships and landingcraft preparing to send thousands of soldiers onto the beaches under massive enemy fire. These soldiers were counting on the guns of the *Arkansas* to improve their odds of survival.

The unnamed sailor goes on:

> The old saying, "The hour is always darkest before dawn" is certainly true, and I believe that particular hour is the darkest I ever witnessed.
> During the blackest hours just prior to early morning light, our bombers began to come over in droves; so that there was a steady hum of engines overhead. Though we could not see them, the sound was a comforting one. There were hundreds of them. They had been bombing the beach head for twenty-four hours before our arrival.[5]

The unnamed *Arkansas* crewmember told of the German fire directed at the Allies' planes in the pre-dawn darkness of June 6:

> The night, black as pitch, would be pierced periodically by tracer fire from the beach—German AA (anti-aircraft) fire, visible from quite a distance. Ignoring this and the heavy AA bursts that threw flak among them, however, the bombers came on, dropped their "sticks" and went back for more. As the bombs hit the beach, the entire horizon would come ablaze with light, like the bright red sun coming up. Time after time the bombers hit, mercilessly, steadily, unerringly, till it seemed there was not a square inch they had missed.
> All this was not confined to the beach alone, for we witnessed dogfights in the air, not being able to see the planes, but by watching the straight, then arching, then sharply-falling lines of horizontal tracer fire. Many times we witnessed a plane go down in a spectacular mass of flames, then the subsequent blinding explosion as the fireball struck the ground.[6]

Young *Arkansas* sailor Richard Kelly described in later years his and his shipmates' understanding of the German fortifications they would be called upon to destroy:

Surrounding the Arkansas were hundreds of smaller ships and landingcraft preparing to send thousands of soldiers onto the beaches under massive enemy fire. These soldiers were counting on the guns of the Arkansas to improve their odds of survival.

Remarkably, in thirty years of service, the Arkansas had never fired a shot in combat, only countless thousands of rounds in practice drills and competitions (often winning awards). This all changed at 0552 hours on June 6, 1944, just as the sky was starting to glow with the coming of the day.

Slave labourers under the direction of Nazi technicians had made of Normandy's shores an adequate rampart for Fortress Europe. High-caliber guns were sheathed in concrete emplacements. Machine gun nests and pill boxes dotted the countryside, together with slit trenches, tank traps and anti-aircraft ditches. Between the high and low water levels on the beaches were several rows of underwater obstacles—hedgehog, tetrahedrons and pole ramps interconnected by barbed wire and liberally sown with mines. Allied planes had hammered these defenses but a heavy artillery barrage was needed to cut a swath, through which the invaders could pour.[7]

Seaman Kelly's notes reflected the tense early morning hours as the *Arkansas* moved into position:

> Behind the *Arkansas*, the gigantic invasion armada filled the channel to the horizon. She had remained undetected, even with the great clanking of her chain as she lowered anchor. Officers in the *Arkansas* CIC (Combat Information Center) anxiously pencilled charts, gun crews sprawled at their stations and lookouts peered at the shadowy shoreline until their eyes ached. In the distance the rumble of the pre-invasion aerial assault was audible. At 0530 the surface around battleship *Arkansas* began erupting with near misses from unseen shore batteries. Turrets buzzed as their electric motors swung them into position: ammunition passers formed their queues. Twenty-two minutes Skipper Richards ordered his guns into action. For the old *Arkansas*, Operation Overlord was underway.[8]

Remarkably, in thirty years of service, the *Arkansas* had never fired a shot in combat, only countless thousands of rounds in practice drills and competitions (often winning awards). This all changed at 0552 hours on June 6, 1944, just as the sky was starting to glow with the coming of the day.

The wait for Captain Fredrick Richards to give the first order to fire had been agonizing to the crew members as they watched German shells fired at them land all around.

> It was quite plain that we were being straddled, and we were more or less apathetically waiting for the "third" salvo that would spell a hit. "Why don't we fire?" was spoken all around the ship. Shortly after I heard the word passed, "In one minute the main battery will fire to port!"...A few seconds later, the entire ship shuddered as the big guns thundered their reply to the paperhanger's [a reference to Hitler's occupation early in life], "Tomorrow the world!" We were prepared for a shock, having experienced main battery firing in practice. However, we had neglected to take into consideration the extra powder charge that accompanies service ammunition, and we were indeed literally raised off our feet.[9]

The Arkansas would spend her first two years of the war ushering ships back and forth between North America and the British Isles, and occasionally into North Africa. Life aboard the ship was as in a bustling city, with a multitude of services required to meet the needs of the crew. The ship's soda fountain had a line at the window when open. Tables in the enlisted men's mess halls stayed busy as different shifts rotated in and out. From USS Arkansas 1944 Pictorial Review, U.S. Navy.

Space was cramped, but the sailors aboard the Arkansas crowded in on rotating shifts to the mess hall, engaging in discussions about home and surely speculation about combat to come. From USS Arkansas 1944 Pictorial Review, U.S. Navy.

*"One of my more distinctive memories was the battleships in action on **D-Day**, they were the **USS** Arkansas and **USS** Texas. It was such a din! They [the Texas] were behind us and these shells would sing their way right over the ship."*

Dave Roberts, a young sailor from Tennessee, wrote of the opening of the battle in his shipboard journal:

At 0600 Arkie opened up with five and three inch battery. Enemy sent up challenge flare to see if we were actually their enemy. They soon found out when our 12 inchers began to speak. Shore battery became a menace with close hit on the Arkie. The Arkie couldn't train on all guns on shore but we spotted the one firing so close but before we got the range they had straddled us with two consecutive shots. The next would have hit us squarely but the French cruiser *Montcalm* scored a direct hit and knocked out the gun.

The *Arkansas* first opened fire with her twelve main guns on a German battery at Longues-sur-Mer, with rapid support of fire from the French cruiser FFS *Georges Leygues*. The combined effort prevented at least that battery from firing upon the thousands of Allied troops that started hitting the beaches at 7:30 a.m. In concert with other bombardment units, the *Arkansas* 12-inchers hurled a tempest of hot steel into pre-arranged targets at Les Moulins, shifting later to points at Ste. Honorine des Pertes and Trevieres.[10]

Seaman Richard Kelly later penned his memories of the *Arkansas*'s initial action as she turned her guns to helping the men coming off the landingcraft under withering German fire.

One of my more distinctive memories was the battleships in action on D-Day, they were the USS *Arkansas* and USS *Texas*. It was such a din! They [the *Texas*] were behind us and these shells would sing their way right over the ship. Some of the targets, I would say, were 8 and 10 miles inland. Every once in a while you hear or see a big explosion way inland and we knew they had hit an ammunition dump or something.

It was such a hectic thing, everybody firing this way, beach fire coming at you. They were firing at us from the pillboxes on the shore. You would hear the shells coming at you. You could hear them whirring by and when you saw them hit the water...well if you were in the wrong place, forget about it. Those German 88s were awful. Once you heard them bark and you were still alive, you knew they hadn't gotten you because that shell would be on top of you before the noise got there.

We did get hit by shrapnel [steel fragments from artillery bursts in the air] every once in awhile. I do remember one incident when we got hit. I was directly beneath one of the gun mounts trying to set up an aid station under gun number 4. As I was coming up the ladder, I heard this noise, and then heard a fellow who was in the gun mount say, "Round and round she goes, where she stops nobody knows." Evidently, a piece of the shrapnel had gotten into the gun mount and wound its way around until it exited. I couldn't imagine how cool he was.[11]

Some of the most sensationalized descriptions of the shelling came in a 1948 Department of the Navy Report sent to Mr. Orville Hancock of Columbia, Missouri:

> An orange tongue of flame licking at the muzzle of a leveled gun, a projectile drilling through a swirling cloud, a deep-throated haroomp, and another shell had been sent in to the German defenses. Arching out from the cannonading ships was a rainbow of whistling destruction, gouging huge chunks out of Normandy, tossing railroad guns like matchsticks, battering gun emplacements out of shape, pulverizing pill boxes.[12]

Some of the hundreds of landingcraft loaded with troops headed toward the Omaha beach passed on all sides of the *Arkansas*. One of the men said, "Invariably troops passing close aboard would wave friendly and shout remarks like 'Give 'em hell!,' 'See you in Berlin!,' and 'Save a few for us!' They are great fighters and gallant heroes, and deserve the well-earned ovations paid to them."[13]

Seaman David Roberts wrote his impressions in his personal journal of the first landings by the U.S. Army on the beaches:

> The taskforce had the shore battery silenced by 07:30 and the army troops started to move towards the beach. The first troops landed about 08:00. The first wave was hit bad. Out of the first 150 men ashore, only eight lived. There were many land mines, booby traps, and machine gun resistance....During the landing hundreds of landing craft were destroyed because the Germans turned their smaller guns (about three inchers) on them.

Anthony Sirco somehow made notes as often as five minutes apart that chaotic morning of June 6:

> **7:47 AM** we picked up survivors from a bomber.
> **7:58 AM** Our fire control party perished when their landing craft caught fire.
> **8:20 AM** we were hit by 6" shell abreast turret two. One shell missed the fantail by 20 feet.
> **9:30 AM** we were firing at gun emplacements in the mouth of a cave. One shell burrowed its way through the side exploding causing a cave-in.
> **1:00 PM** we have fired 64 shells and used 256 powder packets.

At 9:50 that first morning, a British Spitfire fighter flew above the chaotic beaches of Normandy and relayed targeting information to the *Arkansas*, which in turn used it to zero in its big guns on batteries between

"Arching out from the cannonading ships was a rainbow of whistling destruction, gouging huge chunks out of Normandy, tossing railroad guns like matchsticks, battering gun emplacements out of shape, pulverizing pill boxes."

The young sailor from Tennessee, David Roberts, had stood on the deck of the Arkansas and watched the laden landingcraft pass his ship headed toward Omaha Beach. Writing in his personal journal, he also described the landingcraft returning with the wounded, some bound for the medical facilities aboard the Arkansas.

Port-en-Bessin and Colleville. Rear Admiral Carleton Bryant, commanding the bombardment group from aboard the nearby *Texas*, sent an urgent message to the *Arkansas*: "Get on them, men! Get on them! They are raising hell with the men on the beach, and we can't have any more of that. We must stop it!" The *Arkansas* followed the orders with everything its gun crews could muster. By the time the *Arkansas* silenced her guns on D-Day, she had expended 350 rounds of twelve-inch ammunition.[14]

The young sailor from Tennessee, David Roberts, had stood on the deck of the *Arkansas* and watched the laden landingcraft pass his ship headed toward Omaha Beach. Writing in his personal journal, he also described the landingcraft returning with the wounded, some bound for the medical facilities aboard the *Arkansas*:

Around 10:00 wounded were being brought aboard for treatment. The first kid had his right arm shot off. He died a few hours later. One man had his nose blown off because he picked up a booby trap. One sailor was brought aboard. He died in a few hours. He had been taking the depth of the water. While he was on the ocean floor the Germans opened up on the boat he was diving from. The boat got underway. The sailor drowned.

Gunners Mate Sirco penned at 2:45 p.m.:

By this time we destroyed all the targets assigned to us plus an unexpected 6" battery. I got permission to go topside to see what it was like. There were thousands of ships of all kinds. They also brought some wounded troops onboard. Some were horribly mutilated, it was horrible. The British fleet has run into stiff opposition. They ran into 11" inch guns in a shore battery and they have been unable to knock it out as of yet. I thank the Lord that we had the two French Cruisers with us if it wasn't for them we'd have been sunk. We couldn't get to fire broadside the tide kept our bow towards shore so all we could fire was Turret 102. The [French cruisers] went in between shore and us and in 30 seconds knocked the shore battery out. There are now 70,000 troops on shore.

Bragging a bit, Sirco penned later in the day on June 6:

We opened fire, direct hit on second salvo. Direct hit on third salvo. Our plane spotter shot a J.E. 109 down. Direct hit on fifth salvo. From our plane we got word that where the Nazis were concentrated is burning. Direct hit the sixth salvo. Turrets 1, 2, 3 got two direct hits each. Direct hit on the seventh salvo, it demolished some warehouses.

Next came a more somber note, "A hospital ship struck a mine 15,000 yards out."

Nighttime on June 6 offered the exhausted crew of the *Arkansas* little chance for rest. Just before midnight, four German JU 88 bombers zeroed in on the Allied fleet anchored off shore. A primary target was the battleship that had hurled much destruction at the Germans' entrenched forces during the daylight hours.

Two of the bombers broke formation and headed directly to the *Arkansas*, a bad decision for the pilots, as the ship's gun crews knocked both planes from the skies. One of the German pilots, before plunging to his fiery death, was able to release a 250-pound bomb that fell only thirty-five yards from the *Arkansas*'s starboard beam.[15] Seaman David Roberts watched the attack and later that night penned in his journal, "The Nazi air force was out in force from their base at Cherbourg a few miles away. Shot two JU 88's down and the *Montcalm* got one."

Gunners Mate Anthony Sirco penned his observation of the night attack on his ship:

> I was on the topside when a Nazi bomber attacked us. While flying only 200 feet above she dropped a bomb 100 yards off our starboard beam. No damage done except that it threw the gyros out for the night. We shot two planes down.

On June 7, after a night with little rest and the near miss by a German bomber, the crew of the *Arkansas* attacked a battery near Treviers and shelled German troops that were massed near the French village of Vierville. The highlight of the ship's work that day was the direct hit on a railroad overpass just as a train loaded with German troops and supplies was crossing the structure. Intercepted German radio traffic captured the enemy referring to the *Arkansas* as the "Devil Ship"; they vowed that the Luftwaffe would sink her.[16]

Anthony Sirco picked up his journal pen with a first entry at 6:35 a.m. on June 7:

> The Germans counter attacked and set one of our ships on fire. The part of the beach in American hands is a mass of flame and dust from Nazi shelling. We are preparing to engage the Nazi guns. At 6:43 we engaged the Nazis once again. We opened on the Nazis again. Our first shot was a direct hit on a troop concentration.

Each of the nights the *Arkansas* sat off Normandy was a reminder of the Germans' intense desire to destroy the ship that was inflicting so much carnage on their forces during the light of day: "Almost every night Jerry came over and dropped flares all around us, many uncomfortably close. We witnessed Jerry's 'pathfinder' tactics."[17] The flares were intended to frame the ship as a target for German dive bombers and shore guns.

The highlight of the ship's work that day was the direct hit on a railroad overpass just as a train loaded with German troops and supplies was crossing the structure. Intercepted German radio traffic captured the enemy referring to the Arkansas as the "Devil Ship"; they vowed that the Luftwaffe would sink her.

The men serving aboard the
Arkansas had enlisted for up
to four years in the service of
their country, often far from
family and home. One of the
highlights of their weeks at sea
was mail call, such as this
scene from 1944, as the letters
from home were passed out.
From USS Arkansas 1944
Pictorial Review, U.S. Navy.

While guns were manned on
upper decks, meals eaten
below, and letters from home
read, there was a constant
monitor of dials, gauges, and
communication gear deep
within the ship in the engine
room from a crew that had to
be prepared to act on orders
from the commander on the
bridge at a moment's notice.
From USS Arkansas 1944
Pictorial Review, U.S. Navy.

When the sun came up on June 8, the third day of Operation Overlord, the *Arkansas* crew got a request for some long-range action to support the Allies moving further inland. The Allies requested that the ship target German troops seven miles inside France. The response was rapid and effective. The *Arkansas*, anchored off Port-en-Bessin, fired 138 more rounds from her twelve-inch guns, striking in the midst of German troops, tanks, and trucks. "1100 The American flag was hoisted over an area 4 1/2 miles long and 3 miles wide inland," was the proud note in Gunners Mate Sirco's journal on June 8.

Sirco's first journal posting on June 9 came just after midnight and he kept them coming:

> Nazi bombers attacked transport ships. Every ship is firing. The sky is full of tracers. Bombs are firing heavily among the transports.
> **2:30 AM** Three Nazi planes crashed close to us. The Nazis have let some glider bombers go. Glider bombers are radio controlled.
> **8:05 AM** the skipper announced that admiral Bryant and his staff will be on board about 9:00 AM today. Also that we are the only battleship left in this area. The *Nevada*, *Texas* having gone to Plymouth, England for more ammunition. Also that we will anchor only 1 and half miles from shore so that we can have a farther range inland on our guns.
> **11:52** A destroyer is passing us, she was sunk, but they raised her. Her bow and stern stick out of the water while amidships is underwater.
> **8:52 PM** Nazi planes attacked the transports again. I seen two of them burst into flames and crash leaving a black trail of smoke.
> **11:43 PM** Nazi planes attacked us, no damage done.
> **1615** We opened fire. The first salvo was a direct hit. It was a panzer division. The army moved into the town of Liveinne after we routed the panzer division and the German troops.

Even though their shore defenses were pummeled by the *Arkansas*, the Germans had more forces to deploy. As the Allied landings progressed, gaining a foothold on the beaches, the German panzer tank units moved up toward the beaches, intent on crushing the hold the Americans and British had gained. The guns of the *Arkansas*, the *Texas*, and other ships would not allow the Germans a chance of success. The battleships demolished roads, destroyed bridges, and flipped twenty-ton tanks over "as a child does blocks."[18]

June 9 found Sirco's journal pen busy:

> Nazi planes have just dropped some glider bombs. US Destroyers are battling Nazi E Boats which are trying to get into our anchorage. However they did sink two LSTs [shore landingcraft].

The guns of the Arkansas, the Texas, and other ships would not allow the Germans a chance of success. The battleships demolished roads, destroyed bridges, and flipped twenty-ton tanks over "as a child does blocks."

The Arkansas *'s closest call at Normandy came on the night of June 13, the day she fired her final rounds on a concentration of tanks near the French village of Isigny. That night, a German radio-controlled buzz bomb got through the American fleet's jamming equipment and headed straight toward the* Arkansas.

Gunners Mate Sirco began his journal at 4:49 a.m. on June 11 with, "Nazis stopped bombing transports. One plane approached us on the beam, but one shot from a destroyer destroyed it." The lack of further journal entries that day, in contrast to the many over the previous five days, suggests that the pace of activity was slowing for the battleships as the Germans retreated inland.

On June 12 Sirco penned, "U.S.S. Nelson destroyer torpedoed in the stern by a Nazi U-boat." By 9:49 that evening, Sirco had written:

> The battle is unofficially over. 2:00 PM Band played for one hour, marches, popular tunes. All day long they were destroying land mines. The Seabees are still working on their temporary dock.

The *Arkansas*'s closest call at Normandy came on the night of June 13, the day she fired her final rounds on a concentration of tanks near the French village of Isigny. That night, a German radio-controlled buzz bomb got through the American fleet's jamming equipment and headed straight toward the *Arkansas*. The crew urgently worked to find the radio-controlled bomb's frequency. It was a very close call, as the code was found and entered just in time to send the missile into the water only fifty yards off the starboard side of the ship. The near-death experience prompted one sailor to write:

> There are no atheists in foxholes—or on battleships, either! Just as the sky was growing dim, a spine-chilling sound, difficult to adequately describe, filled the air all around us, terminating in a large splash just off the starboard beam. It sounded like an ear splitting whistle. Unconsciously, we all hit the deck and hugged it, bracing ourselves for the explosion. At last, a thousand years later, when it did not come, we cautiously looked up and saw thousands of tons of water settling back down.[19]

Gunners Mate Sirco passed on some bragging by the brass in his notes of June 14:

> It was announced that the Admiral said our shooting yesterday was well done, we were firing at Nazi soldiers only 1,500 yards from our own troops. They said our soldiers were cheering us as our salvos scored direct hits.

How well had the *Arkansas* done at Normandy? Vought observation planes catapulted from the *Arkansas* spotted the targets and relayed locations to the battleship's gunners. So telling was the Allies' teaming of their air-sea facilities that the Nazis were moved to broadcast admission of the fact. Conceded the German radio: "These floating batteries enabled the invaders to achieve overpowering artillery concentrations along the coast."[20]

The confidence in the *Arkansas* was found in a recorded teletype noted by Gunners Mate Sirco on June 15: "Wish you luck. Your enterprise will make history. It will be a fatal blow to the enemy. Signed General Wilson, Admiral Cunningham."

The battleship's work at Normandy was considered done after June 13, for the German forces had retreated too far inland to be reached by the guns of the *Arkansas* and the *Texas*. The work was not yet done in Europe, however, as new orders were at hand.

The *Arkansas*, *Texas*, and three navy destroyers were shifted down the coast of France to hurl their fire upon the German-held city of Cherbourg. The enemy's defenses were at least as formidable as those the battleships had taken aim upon at Normandy. The chief concern of the Allies was the German emplacement that was given the name Battery Hamburg. The fortification was made up of four 280mm guns with steel shields and reinforced with concrete casements. Additionally, the binoculars of the ship's crew revealed six 88mm guns and at least a dozen anti-aircraft weapons pointed out to sea and at the skies overhead. The armament bristling out of Battery Hamburg packed more firepower and range than did the guns of the *Arkansas* and the *Texas*. The powerful German battery possessed guns with a range of 40,000 yards, along with scores of smaller pieces of artillery.[21] It was indeed an apparent suicide mission for the two warships.

Rear Admiral Carleton Bryant, commanding the outgunned Allied fleet, had expected the help of the USS *Nevada*, which had longer-range guns, but found out that the ship was occupied elsewhere. Commanding from the *Texas*, looking out at the *Arkansas*, the admiral ordered the two ships into position 18,000 yards off Cherbourg, at the maximum range of the guns of the old battleships. Upon his command, the ships opened fire upon the still-silent German guns.

Seaman David Roberts chronicled the *Arkansas*'s approach to Cherbourg in his handwritten journal:

> **June 25 02:20** under way, accompanied by *Texas* and six destroyers, 12 mine sweepers. Arrived in first firing position at Cherbourg 10:30 but due to bad weather couldn't open fire until 12:30. *Arkie* opened up first with single barrel fire of 12 inchers to get range on shore emplacements. Shore immediately opened back with heavy barrage. Picked *Texas* as main target first. *Texas* was surrounded by near misses countless times but was hit later on bow. We kept going in and *Arkie* had several misses. Ship was covered with water and shrapnel.

The armament bristling out of Battery Hamburg packed more firepower and range than did the guns of the Arkansas *and the* Texas. *The powerful German battery possessed guns with a range of 40,000 yards, along with scores of smaller pieces of artillery. It was indeed an apparent suicide mission for the two warships.*

The old ship was forced to make do with hand-me-down fire-control equipment, some of which had been taken off the old battleship Tennessee *years earlier. The larger handicap was her gyro-compass, which had been salvaged from the 1930s-vintage cruiser* Tuscaloosa, *a smaller ship than the* Arkansas.

Destroyer was hit three times with light gun shells. Ten killed and seven wounded. All signalmen killed.

Firing the main guns of the *Arkansas* was always a challenge for her crew, but through no fault of those sailors. The old ship was forced to make do with hand-me-down fire-control equipment, some of which had been taken off the old battleship *Tennessee* years earlier. The larger handicap was her gyro-compass, which had been salvaged from the 1930s-vintage cruiser *Tuscaloosa*, a smaller ship than the *Arkansas*. The old equipment simply wasn't designed for the rapid movements a battleship needed to make while exchanging fire with an enemy dug into fortified positions. The ship was instead forced to fire slowly while holding a steady course, giving the Germans a much easier target at which to aim.[22]

The Germans had started returning fire, straddling the *Arkansas* and the *Texas*, splashing shells into the sea on all sides, even scattering shrapnel across their bows, but never quite finding the range for a killing shot, as had been recorded in Seaman Roberts's journal. The battleships were not as successful at shooting at the encased targets as they had been at Normandy, but additional help came from the Allied bombers in the sky. The *Arkansas* shifted her guns toward Fermanville, near Cherbourg, and with but twenty-two rounds decimated four 105mm casemated German guns and their crews. The next day, the port city of Cherbourg was recovered by the Allies, with the remaining Germans surrendering or retreating rapidly.

With the job of taking the strategic port of Cherbourg done, the *Arkansas* was following new orders. She offered up the service of her guns before 7:00 a.m. on August 15, off the southern coast of France between Toulon and Cannes. By 1:00 that afternoon, the ship had moved to fire in support of the Allied landing at Fréjus, assisted by carrier-based planes. The Germans launched an aerial counterattack, with the JU 88s again targeting the *Arkansas*. Splashing bombs into the ocean around her was as close as they could come, however, just as had been the case at Normandy. "1430 One shell hit 50 yards off the starboard bow and three up water spray higher than the ship," noted Gunners Mate Sirco.

After the fall of Cherbourg, the *Arkansas* picked up a new and unexpected task, housing German prisoners. The captured enemy troops were delivered from U.S. destroyers, who had in turn picked them up from landingcraft returning from the secured beaches. Said one sailor, "They were trooped aboard, bedraggled, dirty and obviously happy to be out of the war. We cleaned them up, fed them, and later landed them at a port where they were taken to a prison camp." One German officer was less than humble while aboard the *Arkansas*. He placed his boots in the hallway outside his bunk the first night, expecting his officer status would cause the boots to be returned the next morning, nicely shined. He was irate to find the boots just gone, never to be seen again.[23]

Several months after Normandy, with the *Arkansas* by then stationed in the Pacific, the editor of the *Arklight* came across a copy of a tongue-in-cheek "Hitler's Last Will" penned by a sailor on the ship. Among Hitler's bequests were the following:

> To Japan's Hirohito, I leave all my medals which will help him sink quicker when he goes down.
>   To the GERMAN people, I leave all pictures of myself, especially those printed on soft paper.
>   To Himmler and Goering, I leave the final execution of my will—they are experienced at execution.
>   My final wish is that I be buried in an asbestos suit, as I will need it where I am going.

During the latter part of July 1944, the *Arkansas* was kept in a state of readiness, and the crew suspected that another invasion might be ordered. Docked off Italy, Seaman Roberts penned a journal entry on July 25, "Irving Berlin and part of his cast gave a grand performance on board ship."

On August 11, Gunners Mate Sirco penned from the ship, "I saw the picture *The Fighting Seabees* with John Wayne, Susan Hayward, Dennis O'Keefe." Only weeks earlier off Normandy, Sirco had observed the real Seabees at work clearing mines and building a temporary landing dock.

The tunes of Irving Berlin had hardly faded away when the *Arkansas* became a part of Operation Anvil, the invasion of the southern coast of France between Toulon and Cannes. Seaman David Roberts's journal captured his eyewitness account:

> **August 12** Leave Palermo, Sicily. Ship was sealed yesterday and we were briefed on invasion plans. The *Arkie* will again be the target ship. *Arkie* will move to within 6,000 yards of assigned target which is four 6 inch guns encased with 16 ft of concrete. The worst part of all our ship will be within 9,000 yards of some 9 inch guns which is the *Texas* & *Nevada*'s target. Incidentally, the *Texas* & *Nevada* will stay out from 15,000 to 20,000 yards to fire while we are only 9,000 yards away. Our only hope is that the 9" guns will fire at the other battleships. Invasion will be at dawn Tuesday morn, August 15.
> **August 14** it was announced that Nazi Search Radar has picked us up. We are now 60 miles from Southern France, 50 miles east of Toulon.
> **2127** Three more Nazi search radars have picked us up.

Per Gunners Mate Sirco, the ship was being tracked and targeted by the Germans.

On August 11, Gunners Mate Sirco penned from the ship, "I saw the picture The Fighting Seabees with John Wayne, Susan Hayward, Dennis O'Keefe." Only weeks earlier off Normandy, Sirco had observed the real Seabees at work clearing mines and building a temporary landing dock.

David Roberts, who was born in Mountain City, Tennessee, joined the U.S. Navy at the age of eighteen in 1942. By D-Day, he was serving on the Arkansas as an anti-aircraft gunner. Roberts, with his "lucky number 13" stenciled on the back of his helmet, not only helped repel German bombers but also kept a remarkable handwritten journal during D-Day. Roberts would leave the navy in the fall of 1944 and marry Kathleen Parke, have three children, and spend a twenty-five-year career in New York as an IRS inspector. Roberts died in 1981. Photo courtesy of his son, Dave Roberts.

Anthony Arthur Sirco, apparently called just AA at times, was born in New York in 1926 to a mother from Poland and a father from Ukraine. He joined the navy in 1943 at the age of seventeen, and by D-Day was a gunners mate helping man the five-inch guns aboard the Arkansas. Sirco kept a thorough handwritten journal aboard the ship, through not only D-Day but during the later Pacific battles of Iwo Jima and Okinawa. He survived many navy battles of World War II and joined the U.S. Air Force in 1947. Married in 1951, Sirco was off to the Korean War, and he served in Vietnam in the 1960s. He retired from the air force in 1967 and would support his family as a meteorologist. Sirco died in 2013, a true hero of the "Greatest Generation." Photo courtesy of Sirco's daughter, Annette Knipfing.

Seaman Dave Roberts found time to record in his journal the events of August 15, 1944:

Task Force is in firing position. *Montcalm*, French cruiser, and cruisers *Tuscaloosa* and four destroyers are the only ones in sight of us. The *Texas* & *Nevada* are out on the horizon. The Air Force, Army & Navy are carrying out bombing raids on the beach, very plain to see from our ship. Planes, bombs combined with above mentioned ships and S.C.T.R.s [rocket ships] make a constant rumble which sometimes lasts up to five minutes. Several small Nazi craft were sunk by bombs. The ships did not open fire until 0650 as planned. We bombarded positions until 0800 and then ceased fire as planned. Not a single gun had returned our fire.

Roberts witnessed the success of the beach landings by the Allies:

There were no landing craft obstacles, no land mines and no resistance to the first five waves ashore. The sixth wave reported slight machine gun fire. Out of the first 6 waves of men ashore, there were 15 casualties [compared to the Normandy wave which only 8 men out of 150 survived because of mines and gun fire]. At 1330 the town on the beach sent up a white flag from a tower. We ceased fire and we had expended 32% of our ammunition, 475 rounds.

Per Anthony Sirco's journal late on August 15:

2021 A British Rocket ship came alongside for some supplies. For 10 days all they had was water, biscuits, and margarine.

The *Arkansas* did her duty and survived with only minor damage from shrapnel, in the successful Operation Anvil. By August 17, 1944, the work of the *Arkansas* in the European theater of war was done, for there were no more Germans within reach of her guns. Though the ship had avoided hits from the enemy, she was not without damage. The constant pounding and vibrations from the firing of her big guns had done damage to the old ship. Sixteen of her steel doors or the frames were warped and would not close properly. It was time to sail for the United States, to get some repair work, and to see if a role remained for the oldest battleship in the U.S. Navy in the fight to save the world from tyranny.

Though the ship had avoided hits from the enemy, she was not without damage. The constant pounding and vibrations from the firing of her big guns had done damage to the old ship. Sixteen of her steel doors or the frames were warped and would not close properly.

As June 1944 began, the men
of the Arkansas knew it was
very likely they would soon be
in battle and targeted by
German guns and planes.
Church services were well
attended on the deck, and
prayers were often and fervent.
From USS Arkansas 1944
Pictorial Review, U.S. Navy.

The Arkansas's date with history was near when she moved
into position off Normandy in
the pre-dawn darkness of June
6, 1944. The crew had
declared its readiness to the
ship's captain in chalk in front
of the twelve-inch guns: "You
name it boss, We'll hit it."
From USS Arkansas 1944
Pictorial Review, U.S. Navy.

Inside the ship, behind the big guns, the crew loads the extra large charges of powder needed to hurl the shells up to a distance of several miles in order to hit the entrenched German targets in advance of the Allies' D-Day invasion. From USS Arkansas 1944 Pictorial Review, U.S. Navy.

This photo is of Captain Fredrick Richards, who gave the first order to fire. Captain Richards was awarded the silver star for his leadership aboard the USS Arkansas on D-Day.

The USS Arkansas and
Texas had encountered one
another in places as varied as
the Panama Canal and the
Havana, Cuba, harbor over a
period of thirty years. At
Normandy, the two vintage
warships, both of which had
gone to sea before the first
World War, were teaming up
to do great damage to the dug-
in Germans on the cliffs of
France. The Texas is in the
foreground, the Arkansas a
few hundred yards away, her
guns blazing.

Texas Guns 'keep on the target' while Arkansas fires.

Once the Arkansas and the
other battleships prepared to
cease firing on the beaches,
the vast armada of land-
ingcraft started going by on all
sides, headed for Omaha
beach. As the craft passed,
some of the sailors were heard
to shout down, "Save some
Germans for us!" From USS
Arkansas 1944 Pictorial
Review, U.S. Navy.

Hundreds of the men who headed for Omaha beach on D-Day died, while many others were wounded. Some of the wounded were boosted onto the Arkansas from landingcraft returning from the beaches, where they would be given medical treatment until they could be transferred to other facilities. From USS Arkansas 1944 Pictorial Review, U.S. Navy.

After playing a role in helping the Allies take the key port city of Cherbourg, France, landingcraft passing the Arkansas began offloading to her scores of German prisoners captured in the fighting. The war was over for these men whose short-term home would be the "Devil Ship," as their radio traffic had labeled her. From USS Arkansas 1944 Pictorial Review, U.S. Navy.

The crew of the Arkansas helped process the German prisoners by stenciling in paint on the back of their shirts "PW" for prisoner of war.

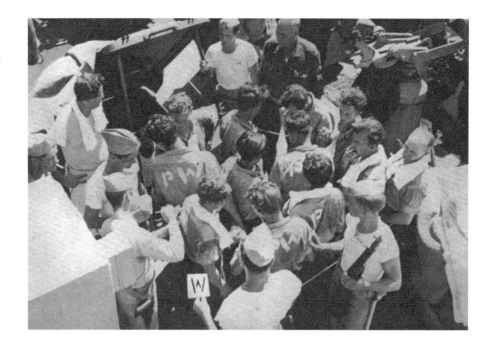

While aboard the Arkansas, one of the Catholic priests serving as chaplain said Mass for the mostly Catholic German prisoners. The ship would later drop the prisoners off at a regular POW camp set up by the Allies. From USS Arkansas 1944 Pictorial Review, U.S. Navy.

In the wake of the success at Normandy, a lot of dress photos were made of the large Arkansas crew in their best uniforms. One of the poses, with their white officer in their midst, showed the segregated black S Division of the ship's crew. Largely relegated to supply and support work, these men also earned the distinction of serving their nation in a world at war. From USS Arkansas 1944 Pictorial Review, U.S. Navy.

By early February 1945, the ships were training off Saipan, preparing to take on the Japanese who had to be cleared from key islands in order to open the path for an expected American assault on the enemy's homeland. The first orders were an attack on a small volcanic speck in the South Pacific that most of the crew of the Arkansas had never heard of, Iwo Jima.

Chapter Seven

War in the Pacific

The *Arkansas* docked in Boston on September 14, 1944, the ship and crew having performed magnificently in helping push the Germans back from the edge of the European continent. By November, she had received repairs, including relining her gun barrels, which had been worn out firing at the Germans. Her crew rested and underwent training for what might be ahead.

After a transport through the familiar Panama Canal, the *Arkansas* tied up at the docks of San Pedro, California, beside her old battle ally the *Texas* as well as the brand-new battleship *Missouri*. The journal of Gunners Mate Anthony A. Sirco chronicled the building sense of apprehension and excitement as the *Arkansas* moved toward the enemy in the Pacific: "1-29-45 we passed through one of the most active submarine areas in the central and southwest Pacific. We are now within range of the Japanese bombers." By early February 1945, the ships were training off Saipan, preparing to take on the Japanese who had to be cleared from key islands in order to open the path for an expected American assault on the enemy's homeland. The first orders were an attack on a small volcanic speck in the South Pacific that most of the crew of the *Arkansas* had never heard of, Iwo Jima.

The suspense began to build once the crew members of the *Arkansas* knew they were headed to Iwo Jima. Gunners Mate Sirco's entry on February 15, 1945, reads, "Two emergency turns were made. The reason is unknown. Later word was passed that a Jap scout plane has radioed our position to Japan. It was picked up at Guam Island."

From February 16 to 19, the *Arkansas* sat off Iwo Jima pounding the slopes of the western face of Mount Suribachi, which rose high out of the black sand of Iwo Jima and on which thousands of Japanese were dug into bunkers and caves. Sirco penned two journal entries on February 18: "We have fired our 1,000th round" and "The U.S. Marines hit the beach at Iwo."

A February 23, 1945, handwritten letter on USS *Arkansas* stationery described one sailor's view of what he was seeing, doing, and thinking when he was off the coast of Iwo Jima:

> Things are pretty good with me. Rather exciting at present. Been shooting at "Japs" a good deal. Find it very much like shooting "dump rats," always plenty of them. By this time you know where this place is and have heard all about it. Iwo Jima, they call it. Never heard of it myself until I woke up one morning and there it was…just like finding a good pond full of trout, way back when. I haven't had a chance to try the fishing lately. Probably wouldn't catch any anyhow. Have seen some pretty good sharks and plenty of flying fish.
>
> Gee, I feel so sleepy right now. The ship is rocking so smoothly I feel as though I were in a cradle. If I could only sleep til noon tomorrow I'd never know there's a war on…. Hell, my ears are still ringing and the dump still has some rats on it.
>
> —Always, Pete

Lieutenant J. G. Fletcher "Ace" Elmore joined the U.S. Navy in 1942, entering as a Seaman 2nd Class. He quickly qualified for the Aviation Cadet program. In November 1944, he received orders to join the *Arkansas* at the Brooklyn Navy Yard, where the last of its repairs were completed to put it back in shape after its D-Day and Operation Anvil efforts invading France. By February 1945, Fletcher was flying the catapulted OS2U Kingfisher observation float planes off the deck of the *Arkansas*.[1]

On the morning of February 19, 1945, when the U.S. Marines were preparing to hit the beaches of Iwo Jima, Ace Elmore was given a key assignment as his plane was catapulted off the deck of the *Arkansas*. He flew high over the landingcraft hitting the beaches, directing firing coordinates back to the ship to communicate where to direct its fire ahead of the marines onto the key Japanese targets.

At 1:30 in the afternoon of June 19, Gunners Mate Sirco noted in his journal, "I was looking through a periscope in the turret to see Jap batteries firing at the L.C.V.P.s and L.C.I.s [landingcraft] bringing troops to the beach." Later in the afternoon, Sirco recorded, "The Chaplain announced that the north end of Iwo has many caves in which the Japs are heavily fortified. We are now going that way to see what we can do about persuading the Japs to come out of those caves."

On February 20, Sirco noted no lull in battle: "All night long gun flashes, fires, bomb flashes, and tracers, star shells could be seen around Iwo." The threat of enemy planes was constant. On February 21, he

Later in the afternoon, Sirco recorded, "The Chaplain announced that the north end of Iwo has many caves in which the Japs are heavily fortified. We are now going that way to see what we can do about persuading the Japs to come out of those caves."

On February 23, from the deck of the Arkansas, Elmore witnessed an unforgettable sight. "I was walking across the deck just having come back from a flight, when I saw Old Glory about one mile away. It was very emotional!" The young pilot had witnessed the celebrated raising of the Stars and Stripes by five brave marines atop Mount Suribachi, the tallest point on the volcanic island of Iwo Jima.

wrote, "Nineteen unidentified planes on our starboard, are firing a.a. [anti-aircraft guns] at them."

On February 22, Sirco penned a sad journal note, "It was announced that we lost the CVE *Bismarck Bay* last night, sunk by enemy aircraft." The aircraft carrier (actually named the *Bismarck Sea*), which had been commissioned only in 1944, had been sunk by two Japanese kamikaze planes the night before in the waters off Iwo Jima, with a loss of 318 American servicemen.

On February 23, from the deck of the *Arkansas*, Elmore witnessed an unforgettable sight. "I was walking across the deck just having come back from a flight, when I saw Old Glory about one mile away. It was very emotional!" The young pilot had witnessed the celebrated raising of the Stars and Stripes by five brave marines atop Mount Suribachi, the tallest point on the volcanic island of Iwo Jima.

Another sailor wrote of what Elmore had observed:

Our special target was Mount Suribachi, a dead volcano rising starkly at the Southern tip of the island. The Japs had fortified it with railroad guns, AA guns, and observation posts peeped out of hundreds of pits and crevices. We gave Suribachi plenty of hell with our main battery for days. One of the biggest thrills of the Pacific war was the moment when the lookouts reported that the American flag was being raised at the top of the mountain—the now immortal scene of the U.S. Marines hoisting the colors.

The flag raising on Iwo Jima inspired a poem in the May 1945 *Arklight*:

THE ARKANSAS AT MT. SURIBACHI:
SO PROUDLY WE HAIL
So proud her bow, her fac'sle bare,
Low in the brine, her waist set so fair
Gliding silent through blackness, a task to do.
Her part: a mission of death, a rendezvous.
Black against the haze of dawn
A cone on this good earth, an evil spawn:
Black ash, molten rock tunneled, it hides
Craven, treacherous—there the enemy abide.
The waters are roughened, shattered the air,
The thunder by day, by night the flare
Of her rifles; a job done well
On this bit of rock, on earth come hell.
Of those green-clad who venture in
To meet with steel, their task therein
To scale the cone and raise on high,
That now we see our standard bright against the sky.
　　　　　　　　　　　　　　　—E. L. Kreis, FLC

Her work in Europe done—hundreds of rounds fired, but not a man lost in combat—the Arkansas *sailed for home. An official U.S. Navy photo, taken from an observation plane, captured the best view of the proud ship in all her glory, steaming across the Atlantic. She would be in Boston by September for repairs and retrofitting. Next stop, the South Pacific, where the Japanese were dug in on a chain of islands.*

At the Boston shipyard, part of the repair needed to get ready to fight in the Pacific was to replace the fifty-foot-long gun barrels of the Arkansas *that had been worn out firing at the Germans in France.*

"Most people think of 5 inch guns as in a turret that fired automatically for anti-aircraft. This was a gun emplacement just like a cannon on the deck. It was nothing automatic."

On February 27, Gunners Mate Sirco penned a half-dozen journal notes, which included the following: "About 100 marines in the nude on Iwo could be seen taking a bath on the beach." "There was an explosion on Iwo that sent clouds of dirt hundreds of feet high on Iwo. Then 9 Navy liberators were observed coming out of the clouds."

* * *

Homer Ellis would return from the Pacific Theater of World War II to go to medical school, becoming a much loved doctor in Fort Smith, Arkansas, where he would help bring several thousand babies into the world. The future Dr. Ellis, however, was but a nineteen-year-old sailor manning one of the five-inch guns on the *Arkansas* in the battle for Iwo Jima.

Four years before his death in 2009, Dr. Homer Ellis gave an oral history interview to the National Museum of the Pacific War, based in Fredericksburg, Texas. The transcript of this interview recorded the memories that had stayed with the successful man his entire life.

Homer Ellis from Biloxi, Mississippi, had enlisted in the U.S. Navy out of high school at the age of eighteen. His first day of active duty was June 6, 1944—D-Day. He recalled thinking on that day, "My goodness, the war is over and I've missed it." Nine months later, he was trained to fire the five-inch guns of the *Arkansas* by the time his ship turned its armament onto the Japanese-held island of Iwo Jima.

Seaman Ellis came aboard reporting for duty on the *Arkansas* in Boston in the fall of 1944 while the ship was being repaired and retro-fitted after its service during Operation Overlord. Ellis said, "It came back to be refitted, had new rifles put in for the 12 inch battery and the ship was just refurbished. It was a mess at that time; we got a lot of new people on board, like me." The relined rifles referred to the fact that at Normandy and the other European beach assaults, the constant firing had worn out the ship's guns, so the barrels had to be relined in order to send it back to war.

The oral history interviewer, in seeking to understand Dr. Ellis's rank and duty, probed as to what he had been trained for, what duty he had on the ship. He replied, "Well, I was a seaman. We called it a deck ape. And that term really meant military common laborer."

Dr. Ellis was a bit modest before going on to explain that his division manned the secondary battery, which consisted of the five-inch guns of the *Arkansas*:

> They were older 5 inch guns. Most people think of 5 inch guns as in a turret that fired automatically for anti-aircraft. This was a gun emplacement just like a cannon on the deck. It was nothing auto-matic. To aim it you had a trainer and an elevator and they turned

little wheels to move it around. It was about as manual as you can be. It was inside an enclosure called an air castle, just a steel enclosure.

The details on how these five-inch cannon-like guns worked on the thirty-year-old ship flowed from Dr. Ellis in his interview some sixty years after the battle:

> It had a casing containing powder and a projectile all in one loaded bullet. You set that on, closed the breech and then fired it. My job, I was the first powder man. They'd put the projectile in it then I pushed that sack of powder [thirty-five to forty pounds in a fabric bag]. Massive amounts of gun powder were stored within *Arkansas* with the bags coming up on elevators behind the gunners as needed.

Ellis recounted his training off the coast of California, where he learned to load and help fire the five-inch guns:

> I'll never forget one of the first times we actually fired that thing, at night, and a guy sent the projectile home and I had this bag of gun powder, and at the instant that I shoved it home, the main battery fired. What I saw was just a flash and I thought I'm dead and gone to hell. A few moments later I realized I'd survived and felt great. They made us wear protective cotton [in our ears], but it didn't do a whole lot of good.

In response to other questions, Dr. Ellis explained that the five-inch guns had a range of about fifteen miles.

Recounting his early months on the *Arkansas* as it stopped off at Pearl Harbor, Dr. Ellis answered a series of questions about the ship: "Wasn't fast, it wasn't that maneuverable. It was old and slow." As to crew, "We probably had 2,000 to 3,000 people on board." "It was a city itself." Asked about the food on the ship, the memories were not good: "Everyone complained. We had a lot of powdered eggs....At that time I had never thought of putting canned cream in coffee; I grew up most of the time having a cow."

As to sleeping aboard the *Arkansas*, Dr. Ellis discussed the hammocks: "That's a trick to learn how to sleep in that and of course I fell out every now and then." Every day, the hammocks had to be taken down and stowed. With enough seniority, Ellis explained, a man was permitted a folding cot, much preferred to the hammock.

By the time the *Arkansas* reached Iwo Jima, American planes had already been bombing the Japanese-fortified rocky island. Ellis explained to his interviewer in 2005 that his gun crew did not really see its targets,

"I'll never forget one of the first times we actually fired that thing, at night, and a guy sent the projectile home and I had this bag of gun powder, and at the instant that I shoved it home, the main battery fired. What I saw was just a flash and I thought I'm dead and gone to hell."

"Each of our trainer pointers [in fire control] had a telescopic sight and I'll never forget one of the guys said, 'Hey guys, they are putting up a flag there on top of that mountain,' and we lined up and took turns looking through the telescopic sight."

that this was controlled by Fire Control above them. They worked with coordinates, which determined where the guns were aimed.

Among the most vivid memories of Dr. Ellis at Iwo Jima was the raising of the American flag atop Mount Suribachi by five marines. "Each of our trainer pointers [in fire control] had a telescopic sight and I'll never forget one of the guys said, 'Hey guys, they are putting up a flag there on top of that mountain,' and we lined up and took turns looking through the telescopic sight."

Iwo Jima was safely in American hands, but it was not long before the *Arkansas* was assigned to perhaps the largest and most difficult mission of the U.S. Navy in the war. It was ordered to the island of Okinawa. A total of 1,213 ships, 564 carrier planes, and 170,000 soldiers and marines were amassed for the assault on Okinawa, the last major Japanese stronghold in the path of the expected campaign against the enemy's home islands.

Between helping win the battle for Iwo Jima and then heading for Okinawa, the crew of *Arkansas* knew that the seas and sky were filled with threats. Some of these dangers were received by CONFIDENTIAL Memorandum on March 6, 1945, and shared with all the crew.

> **SUICIDE ATTACKS BY SWIMMERS** [excerpts from memo]: Indications that the Japanese had resorted to the use of swimmers in suicide demolition attacks upon Allied forces are confirmed by two action reports just received. When search lights were focused astern, [name of ship not mentioned] a large number of Japanese swimmers, estimated at between 30 and 40, were seen approaching. Orders were given to open fire. A small bamboo raft propelled by several swimmers, and believed to have been carrying bombs, was sighted about 200 yards astern. The raft and those Japs were destroyed almost immediately, but other swimmers continued to approach, encircling the ship from all directions simultaneously. All were believed killed by small arms fire except one who dived beneath the surface. He released a demolition charge which caused substantial damage, also injuring the commanding officer.
>
> Approximately three days later, the APA reported attempted attacks by suicide swimmers in LINGAYEN GULF. During a pre-dawn patrol, a picket boat from the APA sighted a small kapok life jacket floating toward the ship. Closer inspection revealed that behind the jacket, submerged but for his face, was a bespectacled Japanese swimmer, clad only in a khaki shirt. The Jap was killed by pistol fire and his body slipped from the jacket, sinking before it could be recovered for examination.
>
> A single picket boat reported killing nine Japanese, all swimming under boxes and most of them officers. They were said to be carrying grenades, booby traps and other small explosives.

On February 16, 1945, the guns of the Arkansas opened up on the slopes of Mount Suribachi, the volcanic peak on the island of Iwo Jima. The mountain is shown rising in the distance, with shells exploding on the slopes. The targets for the ship's guns were the thousands of Japanese dug into bunkers and caves prepared to fire down on the marines who were to hit the beaches within three days after the bombardment had begun.

In a lull in the naval bombardment, the marines headed for the volcanic sand beaches of Iwo Jima by the thousands in their landingcraft, where many would die within the next few hours after this photo was taken. In the distance to the left is the Arkansas. U.S. Navy photo.

Okinawa was the largest amphibious invasion of the Pacific campaign and the last major campaign of the Pacific War. More ships were used, more troops put ashore, more supplies transported, more bombs dropped, and more naval guns fired against shore targets than in any other operation in the Pacific.

The eighty-two-day battle for Okinawa opened with the bombardment from the *Arkansas* and other ships on March 25, 1945, a week ahead of the invasion of the island by the marines.

The battle would be the bloodiest in the Pacific Theater of World War II. Okinawa was the largest amphibious invasion of the Pacific campaign and the last major campaign of the Pacific War. More ships were used, more troops put ashore, more supplies transported, more bombs dropped, and more naval guns fired against shore targets than in any other operation in the Pacific. More people died during the Battle of Okinawa than all those killed during the atomic bombings of Hiroshima and Nagasaki. Casualties totaled more than 38,000 Americans wounded and more than 12,000 killed (including nearly 5,000 navy dead and almost 8,000 marine and army dead). Navy casualties were tremendous, with a ratio of one killed for one wounded as compared to a one to five ratio for the Marine Corps.[2] More than 107,000 Japanese and Okinawan conscripts were killed, and perhaps 100,000 Okinawan civilians perished in the battle. Thirty-four Allied ships and craft of all types had been sunk, mostly by kamikazes, and 368 ships and craft were damaged. The fleet lost 763 aircraft.

According to a report in the Ship's Data Section, "On 25 March the USS *Arkansas* began shelling out the first of 8,721 rounds which that battleship donated to the destruction of the Okinawa stronghold. Anxious officers jammed her plotting room, scanning countless charts and maps for locations of guns, pillboxes and troop concentrations. Her Kingfishers observation planes again transmitted topographical information to the *Arkansas* bridge."[3]

"Ace" Elmore, in his OS2U-Float observation plane, was catapulted off the deck of the *Arkansas* on the Easter Sunday that the land invasion by the marines began; he soon soared over Okinawa looking for targets for his ship. Ace had been assigned one of the large coastal artillery guns that needed to be knocked out before the marines came ashore. As reported in his obituary in 2009, "While searching for the gun, he saw the large barrel suddenly extend out from its camouflaged emplacement and begin to fire on his ship. Directing his ship's return fire at the Jap gun, 'All of a sudden, a giant explosion took place down there. It was like a volcano blowing up, flames shooting out of the top of it. Obviously, we had hit the ammunition dump in the rear of the emplacement. We observed this bitter fire and counter-fire which was directed by us as we circled about 800 to 1,200 feet above the target. This is one of the more exciting moments of my whole Navy career.'" Ace would continue spotting targets around the area for the next six weeks. He was proud of the dispatch sent to his ship from the commanding general of the Seventh Infantry Division, which read, "Congratulations to the USS *Arkansas* air spot for your activities today. Many GI's will be using the return portion of their ticket due to your efforts today. Well done!"[4]

Gunners Mate Anthony Sirco, who had been aboard the *Arkansas* since before D-Day, was at work again with his journal pen off Okinawa: "And the suicide attacks began. Low over the water they came, dozens of them, and the anti-aircraft fire was like a storm in the sky. In seconds a small dot on the horizon would loom as a suicider loaded with bombs on a one way trip." He added, "3-31-45 a suicide plane hit the USS *Indianapolis* and went through the main deck causing considerable damage." Actually, it was the bomb of the plane that heavily damaged the ship, while the Japanese plane carrying it was shot down into the sea. The ship would be repaired and would deliver key parts for the American atomic bomb later in the summer. On July 30, 1945, the *Indianapolis* would be sunk by a Japanese submarine, resulting in the deaths of some 900 of her crew members, the last American ship to be sunk during World War II.

The Japanese made many attempts to strike the *Arkansas*, both from their shore-mounted guns and from the air. One such account was detailed in the May 25, 1945, edition of the *Arklight*, after the battle had ended: "One afternoon during the campaign a light Jap bomber somehow worked its way thru heavy anti-aircraft fire and, flying just above the water, headed straight for the ship. With all the guns of the *Arkansas*, as well as that of other ships, pouring a hail of lead at the enemy, the plane flew toward the ship for an age-long minute. It was a tense moment on the *Arkansas*. Finally the plane faltered, dipped its left wing and crashed into the sea with a tremendous explosion. The wild cheers that broke from the crew were equally as tremendous."[5]

In a lull in the Okinawa battle, Anthony Sirco noted in his journal on April 2: "One of the crew caught a shark and brought it on deck." The writing was decidedly different by April 7: "0730 Red alert, Control Blue 4 enemy planes on the starboard bow. 0753 A Jap plane off the port bow was shot down in flames by a night fighter [P-61 Black Widow]. The fighting on Okinawa is heavy all night long, artillery flashes could be seen. Terrific explosions were heard. Big fires were burning. 2100 Main Battery—commence firing. 2243 Secondary battery commence fire."

Previous suicide onslaughts were almost paltry in comparison to the deluge that ensued: "Starting on 6 April the Japanese 'Divine Wind' blasted the US Navy at Okinawa with a fury never before encountered. *Arkansas* sailors nestled in anti-aircraft gun tubs downed one kamikaze making a dive on the ship's forecastle. Still another suicider careened

"And the suicide attacks began. Low over the water they came, dozens of them, and the anti-aircraft fire was like a storm in the sky. In seconds a small dot on the horizon would loom as a suicider loaded with bombs on a one way trip."

119

Over the course of the battle there were hundreds of kamikaze attacks, several of which barely missed the Arkansas due to the skills of her gun crews. It was reported by the U.S. Navy on April 6-7 that the first use of massed formations of hundreds of kamikaze aircraft called kikusui, *or "floating chrysanthemums," sent more than 100 bomb-laden Japanese Zeros toward the American fleet.*

across the *Arkansas* bow as she and the *New York* were withdrawing after a hard day's pounding of southeastern Okinawa's thicketed shoulders."[6]

The bravery of the crew of the *Arkansas* was not always confined to the ship alone at Okinawa. "Five *Arkansas* volunteers went aboard a stricken LST (a specialized navy craft used to deliver tanks onto beaches) to remove an unexploded bomb which had lodged in her hold. Working under dimmed lights, the five eased the deadly missile from the ship, ended the ticklish business by lowering it gently over the side into 25 fathoms of water."[7]

On April 12, 1945, the Japanese unleashed a last-ditch suicidal effort to sink the *Arkansas*, whose guns were inflicting so much damage on their entrenched positions. "Jap suicide planes, the Kamikazes, the 'Divine Wind' boys were the most dangerous weapons the Japanese had during the last months of the war. The Arky's real taste of their power came with the heaviest Jap air raid of the war, when hundreds of Jap suicide planes came in to break up the naval assault forces that were battering Okinawa defenses from the sea." Over the course of the battle there were hundreds of kamikaze attacks, several of which barely missed the *Arkansas* due to the skills of her gun crews. It was reported by the U.S. Navy on April 6–7 that the first use of massed formations of hundreds of kamikaze aircraft called *kikusui*, or "floating chrysanthemums," sent more than 100 bomb-laden Japanese Zeros toward the American fleet. By the end of the Okinawa campaign, 1,465 kamikaze flights had been flown from Kyushu to sink thirty American ships and damage 164 others.[8]

The battle against the kamikaze attacks inadvertently resulted in the greatest number of wounded aboard the *Arkansas*, as told in the oral history of Dr. Homer Ellis:

> You lay off the beach and throw in shells. But each evening we would go out to this little anchorage and one night a bunch of Kamikaze airplanes came from way over aiming at the *New York*. One was too high but when it flew over the *New York* just kept shooting it. Now as the airplane is going away their line of fire came down right where the *Arkansas* was.

The surprised oral history interviewer could only exclaim, "It hit you all!" Dr. Ellis responded, "We had about 20 guys that got shells. No one was killed but we have had 20 guys who have got purple hearts from friendly fire."

The predawn hours of April 12 captured a lot of notes from Gunners Mate Anthony Sirco for his journal: "One of our own planes was shot down. The Jap plane got away. The flak was so thick it looked like the

Rye Beach on 4 July. A dead Jap floated by." "Jap planes attacked us on the port beam." "A destroyer was hit on the port bow and is afire, burning furiously." The drama only heightened during the daylight hours. "The USS Tennessee was hit by a plane. 22 men were blown overboard, one marine was killed, another seriously burned. The sky is now full of flak. The once clear blue sky is now completely black. I myself saw 14 Jap planes shot down, all were flying low from 5 to 20 feet above the water. Bombs were exploding everywhere."

"2130 A Jap suicide plane just missed our stern by 10 feet, only 44 mm shells were fired at him. And those were against orders."

By 1620 (4:20 PM) Sirco was still scribbling rapid, scrawled notes in the midst of his duties. "Two Jap planes were seen diving on us coming out of the sun. We commenced fire and shot one down, drove the other off." "0830 Picket boats [launch boats of perhaps 50 feet] were hit, two destroyers, one was the Cassin Young, she was hit just aft of #2 turret, most of the fantail was blown apart. The entire forecastle was on fire."

The *Cassin Young* was a 375-foot destroyer commissioned in 1943. She had been named for navy captain Cassin Young, who won the Congressional Medal of Honor at Pearl Harbor. He was killed in the naval battle of Guadalcanal in 1942. One sailor was killed and fifty-nine were wounded in the attack. Prior to being struck, the ship's crew had downed five Japanese kamikaze planes, but the sixth one slipped through. Despite being hit again on July 30 (the last American ship to be struck by a kamikaze attack) and losing more than twenty men, the ship would survive the war. Today, she is anchored as a museum in Boston not far from the USS *Constitution*.

Four days after the massive kamikaze attack, a special memorial service was held on the *Arkansas* to mourn President Franklin Roosevelt, who had died of a cerebral hemorrhage. He had been president for just over twelve years, so long that many of the young men in uniform had no memory of any other chief executive. The service was modeled after the Episcopal service that had taken place at the White House the previous January on the morning of FDR's fourth inauguration.

As reported in the *Arklight*, Chaplain D. S. Robinson asserted that, as president, Roosevelt had wielded more power than any other living man, and went on: "Yet the President was never tyrannical. He used his power for the good of his fellowman, and under a sense of responsibility to Almighty God. He followed the moral motto 'power for the good of others, not power over others.'"

Noting that FDR had been a victim of polio, the chaplain praised his courage in overcoming his physical disability. He said, "A lesser man

Four days after the massive kamikaze attack, a special memorial service was held on the Arkansas to mourn President Franklin Roosevelt, who had died of a cerebral hemorrhage. He had been president for just over twelve years, so long that many of the young men in uniform had no memory of any other chief executive.

The war was over for the Arkansas, as there were just no targets left for her big guns. She would be anchored in the Philippines when the United States dropped the two atomic bombs on the Japanese at Hiroshima and Nagasaki, ending the war.

would have sunk into oblivion. Our President rose above it and became the world's greatest leader." The service closed with a unison prayer for the deceased president.

The *Arkansas* would spend forty-six grueling days off the coast of Okinawa. She fired more than 2,500 rounds from her main battery, more than 3,000 from her five-inch guns, and many more from her antiaircraft guns, especially in staving off kamikaze attacks.

For unexplained reasons, Gunners Mate Anthony Sirco did not pick up his journal writing until June 20, 1945, having not written since April 13. His writings reflected a relaxed crew, visiting Guam and other peaceful stops where the war had subsided and nobody was attacking the *Arkansas*. But watchful eyes were always on the skies, as Japanese planes were still occasionally spotted.

Movie nights were dutifully recorded: "6-28-45 Missed movie *Wing and a Prayer*." "Movie tonight Gracie Fields and Roddy McDowell *Molly and Me*." "6-30-45 Movie tonight *Keep Your Powder Dry* Lana Turner." "7-2-45 Movie tonight *Thin Man Goes Home* William Powell." "7-2-45 Movie *Boom Town* Spencer Tracy, Clark Gable, Hedy Lamarr." "7-22-45 Movie *Hotel Berlin* Raymond Massey."

The movies might have been over for a bit for Gunners Mate Sirco and crew on July 28, 1945, near the Leyte Gulf, as he posted, "0645 We met and destroyed a Jap task force. We were hit by 2 16 inch shells and 6 8 inch shells." The damage was apparently very light. By that night at 1630, the movies were playing again: "Movie tonight Fred Allen Jack Benny."

The *Arkansas* and five other battleships were combined to form Task Force 95. The group was given the task of looking in the East China Sea for enemy activity, of which there was little. The war was over for the *Arkansas*, as there were just no targets left for her big guns. She would be anchored in the Philippines when the United States dropped the two atomic bombs on the Japanese at Hiroshima and Nagasaki, ending the war.

The August 16, 1945, edition of the *Arklight* carried a message from the ship chaplain's column by G. J. Clark, who was reaching out to men who were focused on the war's end and the chance for many to go home: "There's a table in the Crew's Library newly supplied with religious literature—Protestant, Catholic and Jewish. Allow me to suggest, fellows, that you help yourself. You have nothing to lose by a little scripture reading every day or by a little prayer....In fact you have everything to gain. We are in the service of a nation 'under God,' and we have duty then as individuals to be aware of that God and His Providence."

On September 17, 1945, the thirty-third birthday of the *Arkansas*, the ship and her crew found themselves riding out a typhoon off a now peaceful Okinawa, with waves washing completely over the deck. She survived, just as she had survived the near misses off Normandy and the kamikazes. She was soon transporting 800 happy soldiers home to the United States. In what were coined "magic carpet" rides, the ship would make a total of four of these trips bringing home soldiers and marines.

The *Arkansas* settled into port at Seattle on October 15, 1945, just in time for Navy day on October 27. Arkansas governor Ben Laney was present to salute the oldest battleship in the U.S. Navy: "Our pride swells as we say 'Hail' again and a reluctant farewell to the gallant old fighting ship which has brought us undying honor to the name she has so majestically borne these thirty-three years in the United States Navy."[9]

There was much for Governor Laney and the state of Arkansas to be proud of on behalf of its namesake warship. Over the course of World War II, the Arky had sailed 135,000 miles and fired almost 5,000,000 pounds of ammunition. She was awarded four battle stars for her service. Her deeds represented an amazing record for a ship that had first been put to sea in 1912.

The Seattle press, during Navy week, paid special attention to the *Arkansas*. One headline in the *Seattle Post-Intelligencer* read, "ARKANSAS, VET OF FLEET, DOLLS UP FOR FINAL BOW." Another article stated, "America's oldest battleship began her last official public appearance in Seattle yesterday. When Navy week is over, the *Arkansas* will steam south and through the Panama Canal for her last cruise. Next month on the East Coast, she will be decommissioned and scrapped."[10]

The crew of the ship got off a lot of jokes to the reporters about the expected scrapping of their ship. "But we intend to keep up our contact with her through scrap metal razor blades," reported a deck officer to the *Seattle Post-Intelligencer*, adding, "She's the greatest battleship in the world."[11]

The ship's seven combat ribbons were pointed out as part of her "dressed up" final bow. These included the Mexican Service Medal from the 1914 Veracruz invasion, a World War I Victory Medal, and medals for both the Atlantic and Pacific fronts of World War II. "It's her last chance to dress up and she doesn't want to miss it. For all her venerability, the *Arkansas* is just a girl at heart."[12]

In the midst of the celebrations in Seattle, the *Arkansas* crew knew her active service days were at an end, but none of them could have imagined the fate that lay in store for the proud old Arky.

Over the course of World War II, the Arky had sailed 135,000 miles and fired almost 5,000,000 pounds of ammunition. She was awarded four battle stars for her service. Her deeds represented an amazing record for a ship that had first been put to sea in 1912.

123

While the ship was engaged against the Japanese in the South Pacific, the Arklight reflected perceptions of the enemy in cartoons labeled "Japology." The Japanese dug in on Iwo Jima and later on Okinawa would prove to be fierce foes, many of whom fought to the death or committed suicide rather than break their cultural code, which held that surrender was an unpardonable shame on their country.

Gunners Mate Anthony Sirco, who had started keeping a journal aboard the Arkansas before D-Day, illustrated at the bottom of one page the ship's assigned area off Iwo Jima.

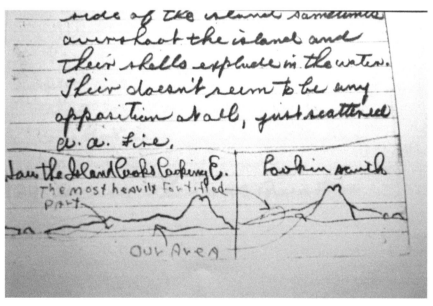

Among the heroes of Iwo Jima were the pilots of the catapult-launched OS2U observation planes that dared the skies and enemy fire over the island to pinpoint targets for the Arkansas guns. In the photo here, the float plane had returned from its mission. Landing beside the ship, it was then hoisted back onto the deck. From USS Arkansas Pacific War Diary, U.S. Navy.

One of the heroes that flew the OS2Us into harm's way to scout for targets for the Arkansas was Lt. J. G. "Ace" Elmore.

125

The photographer captured part of the crew at work around the five-inch guns of the Arkansas. The ship fired some 3,000 rounds from these guns during the battle of Okinawa.

Homer Ellis had started active duty in the U.S. Navy on D-Day, June 6, 1944, at the age of eighteen. Less than a year later, the future physician was helping man the five-inch guns on the Arkansas as the ship sat off shore at Iwo Jima and hammered the Japanese positions in advance of the marines storming the beaches. Photo courtesy of Mrs. Homer Ellis.

Area around the feet of the crew of the Arkansas's anti-aircraft guns was a sea of expended cartridges. Only the constant vigilance and practiced skills of the gun crews prevented scores of Japanese kamikaze attacks from striking the ship that the enemy so wanted to put out of commission.

On April 1, 1945, the raids took on an intense, desperate series of attacks, with the Arky downing one plane headed directly for her forecastle. This photo captured the barrage of flak from exploding shells fired at attacking Japanese planes above the ship. From USS Arkansas Pacific War Diary, U.S. Navy.

Death came to the Arkansas during the battle for Okinawa. Coxswain Peter Paul Konosky died of natural causes on April 12, 1945. With the battle still underway, even with threat of kamikaze attacks, the sailor received a burial at sea officiated by one of the ship's chaplains. When the photo was taken, the crew was honoring the sailor with a salute as his shrouded, weighted body was splashing into the Pacific. Gunners Mate Sirco recorded the death in his journal, "We had a sea burial for a man who died of complications after an emergency acute appendicitis operation. Died 0803 4-12-45."

Just as had the Arkansas crew at Normandy the year before, after battering the beaches with her guns, the crew watched hundreds of landingcraft loaded with marines headed for the beaches of Okinawa. The ship was later there waiting when the landingcraft returned bearing wounded young marines who were brought aboard for medical treatment. From USS Arkansas Pacific War Diary, U.S. Navy.

During a lull in the battle for Okinawa, Gunners Mate Sirco penned in his journal, "One of the crew caught a shark and brought it on deck." The lull was short lived, as the Japanese Zeros were soon targeting the Arkansas.

Jokers Offer Her Baling Wire, But Arky Is a Grand Old Ship

The crew of the Arky got a lot of ribbing in Seattle about having the oldest battleship in the navy, but all knew what a record of service the ship and its crew had compiled. Captain Wade DeWeese, who had commanded the ship, posed with pride next to the ship's bell.

Chapter Eight

Sacrificed to the Dawn of the Atomic Age

The United States and its military leaders knew the bomb worked and knew its impact when dropped on land, on populated cities. There was an unanswered question, however: What effect would an atomic bomb have on a fleet of naval vessels? Did the A-bomb make navies obsolete in any wars to come?

Imagine for a moment, the USS *Arkansas* in the twenty-first century, docked in a special berth on the Arkansas River in Little Rock. Almost the length of two football fields, it would be seen by the thousands of drivers crossing the I-30 bridge every day. Tourists would come from all over the world to see this magnificent ship that served in both world wars and helped invade Mexico almost a century ago.

Alas, while a handful of World War II–era warships—such as the USS *Texas*, anchored near Houston, and the USS *Alabama*, anchored at Mobile—do indeed serve as floating museums, such was not to be the reward for the USS *Arkansas*. Instead, the old dreadnought would play a role in the newly dawning Atomic Age for America's military arsenal.

The world's first atomic bomb, known as the Trinity Test, had been exploded over the empty deserts of New Mexico on July 16, 1945. The next two A-bombs were dropped on Japan—first on Hiroshima and then on Nagasaki—a month later. The devastating impact, with many thousands of deaths, forced the unconditional surrender of Japan and led to the ending of World War II.

The United States and its military leaders knew the bomb worked and knew its impact when dropped on land, on populated cities. There was an unanswered question, however: What effect would an atomic bomb have on a fleet of naval vessels? Did the A-bomb make navies obsolete in any wars to come? Prominent *New York Times* columnist Arthur Krock suggested as much in January 1946, saying that Operation Crossroads "may be proof that a great fleet, including the most powerful modern vessels of war, can...be dissolved" and that "the energy thus released can change the contours of the ocean bed and of distant coast lines." A blaring headline in the *Boston Herald* was even more alarming: "Tidal Disaster, World Climate Change Seen After Bikini Tests."[1]

Among the most avid proponents of testing the new atomic weapons on a navy was Lewis Strauss, slated to become the chairman of the Atomic Energy Commission. In an internal memo to the Secretary of the Navy, Strauss argued, "If such a test is not made, there will be loose talk to the effect that the fleet is obsolete in the face of this new weapon and this will militate against appropriations to preserve a postwar Navy of the size now planned."[2]

Not long after Japan's surrender, it was revealed that those in charge of the Manhattan Project, which had developed the first A-bomb, had discussed "testing" it against the Japanese navy at Truk Island in the South Pacific in late 1944. After the surrender, U.S. senator Brien McMahon of Connecticut made a speech in the Senate advocating testing an A-bomb against the captured Japanese fleet. The chief of the Army Air Force was not convinced, but he hedged his bets by asking the navy to save ten of the thirty-eight captured Japanese ships for possible use as targets, as advocated by Senator McMahon.[3]

The navy, perhaps not trusting the Army Air Force's plan, put forth its own plan, on a bigger scale, in October 1945. The navy envisioned using from 80 to 100 target ships, most of which would consist of surplus U.S. ships.

The drive was on to find out what would happen to warships attacked with atomic weapons. Could any defensive measures be taken? Were the traditional military tactical operations, used in the war that had just ended, now becoming obsolete?

The navy won the contest to see which branch of the service would design and control the bomb tests, besting the efforts of the army, which was relegated to a support role. Admiral William H. P. Blandy was put in command of the task force he personally named Operation Crossroads. In selecting Admiral Blandy, the project got a veteran who had graduated from the Naval Academy in 1913, who had participated in the 1914 invasion of Veracruz, and who had served in both world wars. The highlight of Blandy's career would be overseeing Project Crossroads.

Admiral Blandy was drawn into defending the planned tests, forced to both fend off the concerns of opposing scientists as well as respond to wild speculation among some in the public. He said in spring 1946 before the planned summer bomb tests, "The bomb will not start a chain-reaction in the water converting it all to gas and letting all the ships on all the oceans drop down to the bottom. It will not blow out the bottom of the sea and let all the water run down the hole. It will not destroy gravity.

The drive was on to find out what would happen to warships attacked with atomic weapons. Could any defensive measures be taken? Were the traditional military tactical operations, used in the war that had just ended, now becoming obsolete?

At the end of many discussions, the conclusion was that there needed to be two tests. One would be a bomb set off in the air above the targets, with a second bomb going off beneath the surface of the water where the target ships were afloat.

I am not an atomic playboy, as one of my critics labeled me, exploding these bombs to satisfy my personal whim."[4]

Not everyone embraced the specter of setting off what would be the fourth and fifth atomic bombs in the history of the world. Scientists, including a cadre of those from the Manhattan Project who had built the first bomb, objected to the planned test at sea. At least part of the Manhattan group had stated, even before the bombing of Hiroshima, that rather than dropping it on a populated city, simply running a test for the public might be enough to persuade the Japanese to surrender. There were dire warnings of environmental carnage and the creation of pollution, speculating that "the water near a recent surface explosion will be a witch's brew" of radioactivity.[5]

Although there was little press about it at the time, there was a fatal accident in the preparation of the atomic bombs to be used in Operation Crossroads. Louis Slotin was a thirty-three-year-old physicist who had first worked in January 1945 on assembling the uranium bomb that would be used against Japan. He moved on to work with plutonium, using only two screwdrivers to manipulate two plutonium hemispheres. He knew he had to keep the two hemispheres apart or set off an explosion. On May 21, 1946, while he was working on one of the Crossroads bombs, Slotin's screwdriver slipped, and the hemispheres came too close together. A chain reaction started, causing deadly gamma radiation to burst out of the assembly. Slotin bravely dived into the assembly and tore apart the two plutonium hemispheres with his bare hands, stopping the chain reaction and saving the lives of the other scientists working in the facility. The radiation dose was determined to be approximately what would have been received had one been within a mile of the bomb blast at Hiroshima. After nine days of agony, Slotin died; his death was apparently covered up so as not to cause unfavorable publicity about the atomic testing.[6]

In order to answer questions about the project, the Joint Chiefs of Staff, with the approval of President Truman, sanctioned the Joint Task Force ONE, headed up by Admiral Blandy. There was really only one mission: to carry out an A-bomb test against a fleet of navy ships. The task force was almost large enough to fight another war, as it included some 200 ships, 42,000 men, and 150 assigned aircraft. The forces included members of the navy, Army Air Corps members, and ground troops, as well as a cadre of civilian scientists. At the end of many discussions, the conclusion was that there needed to be two tests. One would be a bomb set off in the air above the targets, with a second bomb going off beneath the surface of the water where the target ships were afloat.

In choosing where to conduct the tests, planners knew that it had to be as remote as possible and in a locale where the residents could be relocated. One site considered by the navy but rejected was the Galapagos Islands, of Charles Darwin fame, off the coast of Ecuador. Eventually, the pin on the map of the vast South Pacific Ocean came down on tiny Bikini Atoll in the Marshall Islands, some 2,000 miles southwest of Hawaii. The Marshall Islands had been captured from the Japanese as spoils of war, and the United States claimed the right to use the remote atoll for the bomb tests.

The Bikini Atoll was deemed ideal by Admiral Blandy and others planning the tests. The atoll consisted of twenty-three small, idyllic islands surrounding a lagoon twenty miles long by ten miles wide, with depths of water at about 200 feet. It was a paradise, but not an uninhabited one, and there lay an obstacle that had to be overcome.

The Bikini Atoll islands were home to 167 people, aptly called Bikinians, and no bomb tests were possible unless these people could be persuaded to be relocated. The task began with Commodore Ben Wyatt, the assigned military governor of the Marshall Islands, of which Bikini was a remote part. Wyatt journeyed to the main village on a Sunday afternoon in February 1946 to put his case in front of King Juda, the leader of the native people of Bikini. His message was that the relocation was needed for the "good of mankind and to end all wars."

Commodore Wyatt used perhaps the only common link between the Americans and the Bikinians, drawing upon the Bible to compare "the Bikinians to the children of Israel whom the Lord saved from their enemy and led into the Promised Land." He concluded what was almost a sermon to the king and his simple people, with this question: "Would Juda and his people be willing to sacrifice their island for the welfare of all men?"

King Juda took the message to his people and after much debate he returned to tell Commodore Wyatt, "We go believing that all is in the hand of God."[7]

God aside, it would be a decision that the king and his people would have ample reason to regret. Relocated first to the Rongerik Atoll 125 miles away, they would have to be moved twice more, each time on the verge of starvation because of poor soil and inedible fish in the surrounding waters. Albeit on a smaller scale, it was a shameful act in the annals of American history comparable to the treatment of the American Indian in the nineteenth century. In actuality, King Juda and his people had no choice, for President Truman had decided the tests would occur at Bikini. King Juda's trust only made things easier for the navy, avoiding potentially ugly press over a forced eviction.[8]

Eventually, the pin on the map of the vast South Pacific Ocean came down on tiny Bikini Atoll in the Marshall Islands, some 2,000 miles southwest of Hawaii. The Marshall Islands had been captured from the Japanese as spoils of war, and the United States claimed the right to use the remote atoll for the bomb tests.

133

The remote, pristine Bikini atoll was selected as the site of Operation Crossroads, intended to test the effects of atomic bombs on naval vessels. The diagram shows the unique shape of the atoll, encircling a lagoon that teemed with life and supported a native population in several small settlements. The target area where the ships were clustered for the two tests is circled.

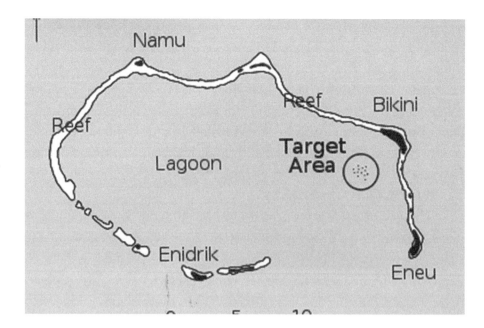

The crew of the Arkansas was housed on the USS Rockbridge outside the Bikini lagoon during the bomb tests. This photograph shows a practice session in which the men covered their eyes upon command to protect their vision from the blinding blast of the atomic explosion a few miles away.

The environmental destruction of the peaceful Bikini lagoon began well in advance of the actual bomb tests, in a process deemed necessary to prepare for scores of ships. Some 100 tons of dynamite were set off in the lagoon in order to destroy the heads of coral that might impede the placement of the ships. Rehearsals for this had actually occurred outside Washington DC using dynamite and model ships in a small pond dubbed "little Bikini."

The selection of the designated surplus U.S. Navy ships to be bombed became a contest of wills between the navy and some states' political leaders. New York and Pennsylvania took note of the fact that the USS *Texas* had been given to its namesake state to become a tourist attraction, and they asked that the ships named for their states likewise be spared. Their requests were denied, and the *New York* and the *Pennsylvania* were consigned to the armada being sailed to its fate at Bikini.

The USS *Arkansas*, the oldest battleship in the navy, was a consensus candidate for the bomb tests, and apparently no requests came from the state of Arkansas to spare its namesake warship. Likely, if not for the Bikini tests, the *Arkansas* would have met the same fate as its sister ship, the *Wyoming*, which was sold for scrap. In reality, if Arkansas had expressed interest in acquiring its namesake battleship, it would have been obvious that the nearly 600-foot-long ship, with its deep draft, could not have been brought up the Mississippi and Arkansas Rivers into the state.

One last-ditch effort to stop the destruction of a big share of the navy vessels came from congressional critics complaining that it did not make sense to destroy ships valued altogether at $450 million. Admiral Blandy was not moved, replying that the true value of the ships once deemed obsolete was only the $10 per ton scrap value, or a total of $3.7 million.[9]

By the start of the summer of 1946, the Bikini Atoll was a beehive of activity as the target fleet was moved into position in the lagoon. That target fleet included four obsolete battleships, including the USS *Arkansas*; two aircraft carriers; eleven destroyers; eight submarines; and an assortment of smaller vessels, along with three surrendered German and Japanese ships. Those target ships were equipped with fuel, ammunition, and an array of scientific instruments intended to measure things like radiation, air pressure, and ship movement. To test the effects on living flesh, some of the ships carried live animals, including 200 pigs, 200 goats, 5,000 rats, and even grain stores infested with insects. The plan was to later have the National Cancer Institute study the offspring of any surviving insects for genetic effects of radiation.[10]

Use of living animals in the planned tests drew a backlash from people tracking the story in the press. Admiral Blandy responded to the protests: "We regret that some of these animals may be sacrificed but we

If Arkansas had expressed interest in acquiring its namesake battleship, it would have been obvious that the nearly 600-foot-long ship, with its deep draft, could not have been brought up the Mississippi and Arkansas Rivers into the state.

Having spent the first part of 1946 at San Francisco, the Arkansas for the last time steamed away from the United States, which she had defended for more than three decades. She stopped briefly at Pearl Harbor before her last sail for Bikini. Once the grand old ship entered the clear blue waters of Bikini's lagoon, her fate was sealed.

are more concerned about the men and women of the next generation than we are about the animals of this one. The Army and Navy simply can't be starry-eyed about this phase of the experiment." Each of the animals, even the rats, was tattooed with a number. The pigs, whose skin most closely matched that of humans, were to be dressed in navy anti-flash suits and smeared with anti-flash lotion.

A Conservative party member in London wrote of the use of animals: "Why choose innocent animals when there are so many guilty men available?" Members of the Southern Dairy Goat Owners and Breeders Association came to Washington to protest the tests, saying, "Good goats are scarcer than good Congressmen." Admiral Blandy's only concession to the protests was a decision not to use dogs as test subjects.[11]

What was not foreseen were offers that came from people volunteering to be used as human subjects in the atomic bomb tests, at least eighty-five of them. One volunteer pointed out that the navy had no plans to test the bomb on alcoholics. "Fifty percent of our population are alcoholics and as an alcoholic I offer myself as a guinea pig. Do not think of this as murder because I am willing to sacrifice my life to science. I am worthless anyhow." However, the man added a postscript, "I'll bet you $1,000 I live." Other human volunteers included a nineteen-year-old marine who had served on Iwo Jima, a navy man saying he was dying of diabetes, and a Washington State prison inmate hoping to "pay [his] debt to society."[12]

Having spent the first part of 1946 at San Francisco, the *Arkansas* for the last time steamed away from the United States, which she had defended for more than three decades. She stopped briefly at Pearl Harbor before her last sail for Bikini. Once the grand old ship entered the clear blue waters of Bikini's lagoon, her fate was sealed. A fleet numbering almost 100 target vessels of all sizes was gathered into the Bikini lagoon. More than twenty target ships were anchored within the target cluster, within 1,000 yards of a kind of bull's-eye for the first planned test, the aerial explosion to be labeled Test Able. The ships that survived would become targets for the next test, labeled Baker, in which a bomb would be set off beneath the surface of the sea.

The preparation work in the weeks leading up to the test involved training 42,000 men to service the operation. It took some 150 ships to house all the men, supplies, and test equipment needed for the project. Just placing the instruments, 10,000 in total, took weeks and many hands to prepare for the bomb tests. Instruments including cameras were placed on the target ships, ashore on Bikini, underwater, and some even in drones set to fly through the expected mushroom cloud, something never done in the history of mankind.

By the time the tests were completed, the cameras would snap some 50,000 still photos and 1.5 million feet of movie film. At the time, it was estimated that half of the world's film supply had been shipped to Bikini to document the Crossroads tests, which would make it the most photographed event in the history of the world up to that time.[13] Some of the cameras were mounted in eight radio-controlled B-17 bombers, surplus planes literally converted to large unmanned drones carrying not only automatic cameras but also radiation detectors. The unmanned but well-equipped planes would be able to fly through mushroom clouds, an act that would be fatal to human pilots.

Test Able

Once they helped position the ship within the target area, the crew that had sailed the *Arkansas* from Hawaii to Bikini was relocated to the USS *Rockbridge*, which would serve as a floating barracks for the crew during the tests. Among the sailors who had helped get the *Arkansas* across the Pacific for her date with the atomic age were two young sailors who would later retire to Hot Springs, Arkansas. The authors were privileged to have been able to interview James Elliott and Bill Ringgold in the spring of 2011 in preparation for this book. Ringgold, born in 1926, had joined the navy in 1944. Elliott, born in 1927, had joined earlier in 1944; he first saw service on an aircraft carrier and served on five different ships over a twenty-four-month period.

James Elliott first met Bill Ringgold when he came aboard the *Arkansas* in December 1945 and ended up working for him in the ship's bakery. The two men served aboard the ship while it crossed the Pacific to return soldiers and marines home from the former battlefields, in what came to be called the "magic carpet runs." Elliott recalled being in a hurry one day, dashing across the deck and very nearly running over the sunbathing commander of the ship, Captain Wade DeWeese.

Seamen Elliott and Ringgold, before they arrived at Bikini, were given printed instructions and orders to be followed in preparing for the bomb tests, as well as what to expect during and after the actual explosion. The sailors were told they would watch the actual bomb drop. Sixty-five years later, the two men passed on to the authors a copy of the instructions given to the sailors.

Queen Day, the practice drill, was set to occur eight days prior to the dropping of the bomb. A key test would be the ability to remove the crew from all the target ships, ensuring that not a single man was left aboard any of the ships to be in the path of the atomic bomb. The printed instruc-

At the time, it was estimated that half of the world's film supply had been shipped to Bikini to document the Crossroads tests, which would make it the most photographed event in the history of the world up to that time.

137

"The ship will be placed in Condition Zebra. No personnel will be left on board. The last person to leave the ship will be the Captain. Anyone finding himself left in the ship shall haul down 'Yoke' and hoist all the flags available."

tions were detailed and were expected to be closely studied by the sailors, stating items such as, "Each man will carry a life preserver, mattress and bed linen. On leaving the ship all magazines, storerooms, etc. will be unlocked. The ship will be placed in Condition Zebra. No personnel will be left on board. The last person to leave the ship will be the Captain. Anyone finding himself left in the ship shall haul down 'Yoke' and hoist all the flags available." The USS *Rockbridge* would be the *Arkansas* crew's floating home for the balance of the bomb tests and then was to take up an eighteen-mile circle pattern around the planned site of the bomb drop.

The navy's instructions to the men of the *Arkansas* next stated what to expect on the actual day of Test Able:

> On Able Day all men will be called on deck at an appropriate hour to view the explosion. It should be remembered that the atom bomb explosion will be of tremendous force; the blast will be longer and heavier (you will feel it at 20 miles); the flash will be brighter (it can damage your eye retina at 20 miles); the heat generated can "sunburn" your skin. At a distance of 20 miles these effects will be less, *but* all precautions must be taken and orders for viewing the bomb will be given over the P.A. system. Ten minutes before the expected drop (How Hour) all personnel will assemble on deck; at 5 minutes before the drop, the Commanding Officer will re-read the safety precautions; with two minutes to go all personnel without *specially authorized* goggles will face away from Bikini, look down at the deck, shut their eyes and cover their *closed* eyes with their bended arm. Immediately after the flash all personnel may carry on and watch the rest of the show. Remember that at 20 miles your eyes can't be damaged, but the initial flash is so bright that you will be blinded for several minutes and will not see the mushroom cloud, and ball of fire, or the incandescent column.

The instructions given the sailors next went on to project the required tasks after the aerial atomic bomb had exploded and the mushroom cloud had vanished into the atmosphere:

> It is expected that after Test Able explosion some ships in the center area will be sunk, some sinking, some on fire and some heavily damaged. It is hard to estimate what the exact situation will be when personnel re-enter the lagoon; but the responsibility for seeing that ships are safe for reboarding rests on initial boarding teams composed of specialists in salvage and radioactivity; therefore we may all rest assured that no dangers exist when the ship's boarding teams reboard, except those situations created by our own carelessness.

The reboarding teams were to be labeled A, B, C and D. Teams A and B would go first after the specialists had given the green light. "All men returning in Teams A and B will wear green clothing, gloves, field shoes, and belts; carry flashlights, canteens, kit bags with food, and several sheets of toilet paper."

It should be remembered, in reading all the assurances that the irradiated ships would be safe, that the world had scant experience at that point with the aftermath of an atomic bomb. Only three had been exploded, all over land, none at sea. The authors of the twenty-three pages of instructions given sailors Elliott, Ringgold, and the other personnel were seemingly oblivious to the danger of freshly irradiated ships, as the flyer went into detail about what to do after boarding the expected heavily damaged ships still afloat: "Make a preliminary survey of damage, fight topside fires if necessary, clear away debris, inspect turrets and topside ammunition, and bring all damage to the attention of Lt. Powers (Damage Control Officer)." Lt. Powers would act almost as a referee, making the calls on what was safe to proceed with and what was not.

Team B's assignment was to follow Team A, open up and inspect the inside of the ships, and "make the ship habitable for Teams C and D." These latter teams were to consist of engineers, damage observation officers, and army personnel. The handouts to the crews listed all the teams by name and rank.

In a retrospective reading decades later, it challenges logic that in a ship just damaged by an atomic bomb, the engineers were to "Make the machinery operable, with priority to lights and ventilation" among other assignments—all this so that the surviving and somewhat restored ships could then be likely finished off by the planned second atomic bomb, Test Baker.

James Elliott was assigned to D Team 2, Bill Ringgold to D Team 9. As the preparations and practices went forward in advance of the big day, the men expected from the paperwork that they would board a damaged ship, a ship they presumed would be the *Arkansas*, well after it had been cleaned and stabilized. Circumstances would dictate a much different mission for them, as it turned out.

On July 1, 1946, Test Able was carried out after weeks of planning and practices. The bomb was dropped from the B-29 Superfortress *Dave's Dream*, a plane that was renamed from the previous moniker *Big Stink*. The bomb detonated as planned at 520 feet above the target fleet, creating a great fireball across the horizon clearly visible from the observing ship-based personnel some twenty miles distant.

The resulting damage was less than many had predicted, with only five lesser ships sunk, one of those a Japanese cruiser that did not go down until the following day. The damage was too light for some of the

139

114 members of the press who had been allowed to observe. The navy offered the theory that perhaps heavily armored ships were just hard to sink unless damaged below the water line.

The actual reason for the lighter than expected damage eventually emerged, however, and it had little to do with the armor on the ships. The bomb had actually missed its target by 710 yards, totally missing its prime target, the battleship *Nevada*.

Once the inspection teams went into the lagoon, it became clear that while most ships had not sunk, there was widespread damage from the bomb's air-pressured shockwave. Of considerable interest was the fate of the Japanese battleship *Nagato*, from which the 1941 attack on Pearl Harbor had been commanded. It was the only large ship inside the 1,000-yard radius, but it sustained only moderate to light damage.

The USS *Arkansas*, while still afloat, suffered a lot of damage to her upper structure, with some oily fires breaking out at various points. Not visible to the eye, however, was the radiation the old ship picked up. The *Arkansas* was one of three major ships within a half mile of the bomb denotation, so it drew a closer inspection than others. A pool of water that had washed upon the deck was measured for radiation and found to have eight roentgens per eight hours, the most found on any of the tested ships.[14]

James Elliott and Bill Ringgold, the young sailors who would eventually go on to live in Hot Springs, Arkansas, had been on the deck of the *Rockbridge* when the bomb dropped, shielding their eyes as instructed. Years later, they offered the opinion that they were much closer to the explosion than the reported twenty miles, perhaps as close as twelve miles by their estimates. They did have a spectacular view of the mushroom cloud slowly dissipating into the sky, once they turned their faces toward where they knew their old ship, the *Arkansas*, was anchored on the distant horizon. They assumed at that point that they would be at some leisure for several days until called on as part of Team D, the last ones to board the damaged ships.

Elliott and Ringgold related that they were standing on the deck three hours after the bomb blast with other sailors watching the smoking fires and haze in the distance when the ship's captain came by asking for volunteers to go aboard the *Arkansas* to fight fires and begin a cleanup. It was unclear in retrospect exactly why these instructions deviated from the preprinted plans. Per both Elliott and Ringgold, nobody raised their hands to volunteer. Repeated assurances that there was no danger from radiation aboard the recently targeted ships still prompted no volunteers among the men, who could see the black smoke rising on the horizon where the ships lay at anchor. The captain, hands on his hips, did not wait long before pointing down the line, "You, You, You, and You." By the time he finished, young Elliott and about 100 other sailors were headed in a launch for the *Arkansas*, which only hours earlier had been blasted by an atomic bomb. Ringgold would join his friend three days later on the irradiated ship.

As their launch neared the battered *Arkansas*, the damage to her upper structure, which was twisted and broken, was apparent to Elliott through the black, oily smoke rising from numerous fires burning on the ship. The damaged and radioactive ship was to be the home of the crew for the next three weeks. The two sailors vividly remembered spending the first three days struggling to put out fires. The young men, fastened together for safety with a rope, moved back and forth through the thick smoke, aided by a single flashlight. No protective clothing had been offered to them. They could only hope as they mopped and scrubbed away the dust and debris from the bomb that the assurances of safety they had been given were accurate.

It was a challenge to fight the fires with the equipment furnished. Elliott described it this way: "We fought the fires with high-pressure pumps, adding a mixture in front of the pumps that had four sailors dumping powder to make foam. We had to have foam to fight the oil fires, and we had to have a large pump to pump water back out to the lagoon, and that is what was used to make our drinking water, and to bathe. The drinking water tasted like diesel. As of today, I still have trouble drinking water."

The official navy records in the wake of the first bomb, Test Able, as well as the second three weeks later, Test Baker, showed no injuries or fatalities among the thousands of servicemen participating in Operation Crossroads. James Elliott, breaking his silence after more than six decades, said there was indeed a fatality, a man who had been left behind aboard the *Arkansas* before Test Able.

Elliott's memories are as follows:

> There were about 100 of us that was sent back to the *Arkansas* about three hours after the bomb was dropped. After three days on the ship looking for fires we found a sailor sitting in the brig, dead, who had been left aboard the ship before the bomb was dropped. I had testified against him for hitting the lieutenant. We found him in the brig with his elbows on his knees and his head in his hands. We were sworn to never tell what we found not even in fifty years. I used to remember the name of the sailor in the brig and the officer but due to the time it happened and my age I have forgotten. Sometimes they come to me in my nightmares but when I wake up I don't remember the names.

The official navy records in the wake of the first bomb, Test Able, as well as the second three weeks later, Test Baker, showed no injuries or fatalities among the thousands of servicemen participating in Operation Crossroads. James Elliott, breaking his silence after more than six decades, said there was indeed a fatality, a man who had been left behind aboard the *Arkansas* before Test Able.

This photo of the Arkansas was taken several days after the aerial Test Able, after the initial cleanup crews had put out the oily fires that broke out after the blast. Looking at this photo in 2011, Jack Freeze of Fort Smith—who, at the age of eighteen, went aboard the ship several days after the blast—talked of his memories: "Great photo. Soon after it was taken we were washing the weather decks. That's when we had all the water running aft and filling the hole in the melted deck. My sleeping compartment was right under the damaged deck—eighteen-year-olds can sleep anywhere." Hundreds of sailors stayed aboard the damaged ship preparing it for the second bomb, Test Baker.

James Elliott was born in Rio Hondo, Texas, in 1927, and joined the navy in November 1945, after World War II had ended. The eighteen-year-old sailor had not missed an adventure, however, because he found himself in 1946 as part of the crew sailing the Arkansas to its atomic destiny. While cleaning up the irradiated ship after the first atomic bomb test at Bikini, Seaman Second Class Elliott suffered severe scald burns to his feet, an injury that would take a year to heal. After his navy service, Elliott attended college under the GI Bill, obtaining expertise in electronics. (After a career as a television repairman, he retired to Hot Springs, Arkansas, where he was kind enough to contribute his memories to this book before his death in 2013.)

There has never been any published account of a sailor left behind, or of any fatality at Bikini, nor have the authors found any other source to confirm what Elliott reported. Be that as it may, in the words of James Elliott: "I was there, and I told the truth!"

James Elliott recalls that after three days, the crew had doused the oily fires on the *Arkansas*, at which point he was joined by his friend Bill Ringgold. Knowing they would be living on the ship for next two or three weeks, they proceeded to get the ship's bakery in the mess hall back in service. The men would spend the next three weeks, when not minding the bakery, scrubbing the radiation dust and debris from the ship's deck.

As to the bakery on the wrecked *Arkansas*, Ringgold said, "Most of us were ordered to go back on board the ship three hours after the bomb dropped, to put out fires and to bake bread, cakes, and other pastries with all the same supplies that were left on the ship before the bombing."

Jack Freeze, who would later be mayor of Fort Smith, Arkansas, was a year out of high school when his navy hitch put him on the *Arkansas*, headed to Bikini and Operation Crossroads. He was stationed on the *Rockbridge*, as were Elliott and Ringgold, before the first bomb. He said, "After the first test we stayed out to sea on the assigned APA, a small transport boat. There was a small number of radio-controlled boats that were measuring the radioactivity in the target area daily." By the time Freeze went aboard the *Arkansas*, some days after Test Able, the fires were out and the cleanup was under way. He said:

> When we went aboard, the fantail had been melted by the bomb heat and it looked like a small pool. The Arky crew began to scrub down the wood deck, and all the water traveled back to the fantail and became a large pool. We had to figure out a way to siphon the water out of there. Being a native Arkansan, I knew how to siphon. I suggested we take a small length of fire hose and prime it with a bucket of water and then drop one end in the deck water and throw the other end over the side. Worked like a charm.
>
> Second Class Garnor, who was on the boat crew with me, and I both fell into the beautiful deep blue water of the lagoon and got radioactive. We were sent immediately to shower and report back to the Quarter-deck for a Geiger Counter test. It was negative. We were told that it was possible that we would be sterile or lose our teeth and hair. We were asked to notify the navy if anything like that occurred. I married and we have four healthy children.

The cleanup crews likely took little solace from the fate of the goats, pigs, and rats that had been confined to the target ships before the bomb was dropped. The purpose of the animals' presence was to test the damage the bombs would do to living creatures. An estimated 35% of the

The cleanup crews likely took little solace from the fate of the goats, pigs, and rats that had been confined to the target ships before the bomb was dropped. The purpose of the animals' presence was to test the damage the bombs would do to living creatures.

One featured survivor was pig #311, which was found swimming in the lagoon after the blast. The pig had been locked in the officer's toilet aboard the captured Japanese cruiser Sakawa, which sank in the wake of the bomb, yet the animal somehow escaped.

animals died as a direct result of the blast or radiation exposure. The animals close enough to the single pulse of radiation from the bomb blast died, while those farther away survived.

One featured survivor was pig #311, which was found swimming in the lagoon after the blast. The pig had been locked in the officer's toilet aboard the captured Japanese cruiser *Sakawa*, which sank in the wake of the bomb, yet the animal somehow escaped. The lucky pig was brought back to Washington DC to live out his life in the Smithsonian Zoo. A year later, the pig had grown to 350 pounds and was apparently healthy as to his blood levels. He was found to be sterile, however, so he had not escaped Bikini undamaged by the radiation.

The impact of the radiation on living flesh was evaluated on the USS *Nevada*, the epicenter of the target (though missed by nearly a half mile). The ship was not sunk and was tested to be little contaminated by radiation. One goat had been tethered inside a gun turret shielded by armor plate; it died four days after the blast of radiation sickness. This told the navy that if it had been a fully manned ship, one enemy atomic bomb dropped a half mile away would have made the ship a floating coffin.

Test Baker

After three weeks of first fighting fires and then literally scrubbing the decks of the *Arkansas* with mops and brooms, Elliott, Ringgold, and the rest of the crew left the ship; this was the final time men would ever trod her wooden decks. They returned to the USS *Rockbridge*, where they would witness the second atomic bomb test, Test Baker. This bomb would be detonated approximately ninety feet below the surface in a part of the Bikini lagoon measuring a total depth of 180 feet.

On the morning of July 25, Elliott, Ringgold, and hundreds of others gathered on the deck of the *Rockbridge*, looking out toward the ships remaining from Test Able, including the *Arkansas*, where they had lived for the past three weeks, cleaning up from the first bomb. With the exception of the ship from which the bomb was suspended, the *Arkansas* would be the closest ship to the detonation. Sailors like Elliott and Ringgold knew that there would be no fires to fight nor decks to scrub on the *Arkansas* after this next bomb was set off.

The photographs of the Baker explosion were at the time unique compared with nuclear detonation photos previously taken. There was no blinding flash to obscure the target area, as the explosion itself was largely unseen. What was starkly visible was the towering column of water, dwarfing the huge ships and showing the power and scope of the mushroom-shaped fountain of seawater.

The underwater fireball from the bomb took the form of a rapidly expanding hot gas bubble that generated supersonic hydraulic shock waves that literally crushed the hulls of nearby ships as it spread out. Farther out, the waves began to slow, at first to the speed of sound in water, approximately one mile per second. The slowing impact allowed ships farther from the site of detonation to stay afloat. Later tests on the sea floor found a crater thirty feet deep and 2,000 feet across.

Press observers who watched Test Baker shared the most vivid reactions.

"A gigantic dome of water, white, beautiful, terror-inspiring, at least a mile wide, rose nearly a mile in the air immediately," said Philip Porter of the *Cleveland Plain Dealer*. Journalist William Laurence's dispatch read, "For a time it looked as though a giant continent had risen from the sea, as though we were watching the formation of a continent that had taken place when the earth was young, and then it took the shape of a giant chain of mountains, covered with snow, glistening in the sun."[15]

The observers noted some major differences between the Test Able aerial detonation and the underwater one of Test Baker, with these differences confirmed by later testing with various instruments and evaluation of photographs. In the second test, the damage to the target ships came from below from water pressure, not from the air pressure shock waves as were seen from Test Able. The most vivid, meaningful difference became apparent when tests found how contaminated with radiation the surviving ships were from the poisoned seawater that washed over the decks in the wake of the massive water plume. Even after the waves subsided, a fine radioactive mist continued to coat every ship in the lagoon. Most of the surviving vessels were found to be impossible to decontaminate, despite efforts to do so, and were later intentionally sunk.

The 27,000-ton *Arkansas*, given that it was only 225 yards from the detonation, would have had no chance of survival. For the first two seconds of the blast, the view of the ship was blocked by the erupting geyser of foaming water. As seen in photos, the *Arkansas* was then a black ship-shaped dot at the bottom of a massive tower of seawater. The underwater shock wave crushed the starboard side of its hull and rolled the battleship onto its side.

Accounts of witnesses vary regarding how long it took the *Arkansas* to sink, but it took only seconds. The 562-foot ship, three times as long as the lagoon was deep, seemed to lift straight up, its bow pinned to the sea floor, its stern protruding 350 feet into the air. With what would have

The most vivid, meaningful difference became apparent when tests found how contaminated with radiation the surviving ships were from the poisoned seawater that washed over the decks in the wake of the massive water plume. Even after the waves subsided, a fine radioactive mist continued to coat every ship in the lagoon.

been, in the literary imagination, a mighty groan, the *Arkansas* then toppled backward into the water, topside down.

The old dreadnought the *Arkansas*—only lightly damaged by the enemy in two world wars, despite near misses by German batteries at Normandy and close calls from Japanese kamikaze dive bombers in the South Pacific—had been sent to the bottom of the sea by its own U.S. Navy.

The Arkansas newspapers covered the atomic tests at Bikini, as did all of the U.S. media. The day after Test Baker, the *Arkansas Democrat* offered this editorial:

> The two atomic bomb tests made at Bikini were planned to determine what man's most destructive weapon would do to navies. The gallant old battleship *Arkansas* was the only capital ship [meaning major ship] sunk by Wednesday's underwater explosion....Both bomb tests have at least proven that navies of the future will be, to say the least, heavily handicapped by the bomb in the hands of the enemy....One fact seems certain. Great numbers of battleships cannot be concentrated in small areas say to cover landings of troops....The most-hoped-for effect of the Bikini tests is that they will impress upon the nation's leaders the necessity of settling differences through tolerant discussions. Peace now as always can come only when men want it in their hearts."[16]

The effects of the radiation released in the two atomic bomb tests, and the effects on the cleanup crews, would be researched and debated for many years to come. In Test Able, much of the released energy and radiation went up into the atmosphere and dissipated. With the underwater Test Baker, however, a huge amount of radioactive material collapsed back into the lagoon and rained down onto the target vessels.

In the immediate aftermath of the second bomb's detonation, it became clear that the navy had no workable cleanup plan. Even though the surviving ships were coated with a radioactive mist that settled over the entire area, the navy sent men to clean the surviving ships with traditional deck-scrubbing methods of hoses, mops, brushes, soap, and lye. Even fire boats, which had been too close to the contaminated ships so that their crews were drenched with radioactive spray, were used. Film badges worn by the crew to measure radiation exposure indicated that over three days in early August 1946, there were sixty-seven overdose cases. The majority of Geiger counters deployed quickly shorted out, making even the weak effort at monitoring radiation levels a failure.

In the midst of the often futile cleanup efforts following Tests Able and Baker, Jack Freeze—the future mayor of Fort Smith, Arkansas—also spent time on a small boat that delivered the mail and movies among the armada of ships that lay out of range of the tests, housing technicians and sailors. He recalled, "One day I looked down and saw the USS *Saratoga* under water. You could see the flight deck. The clear blue water made it look like it was shimmering. A ghostlike view." The massive aircraft carrier *Saratoga*, which had been launched in 1920, had been sunk after Test Baker.

It may have been the contamination of the lagoon, more even than the ill-equipped crew, that convinced Admiral Blandy that cleanup was a hopeless mission. A live, and seemingly healthy, surgeonfish was captured by the scientists working in the aftermath of the bomb tests. The fish had eaten contaminated algae and absorbed plutonium into its scales, allowing the fish to literally make its own x-ray.

The negative publicity of the failed cleanup was enough to cancel the next planned atomic bomb test in the area, Test Charlie, which had been planned for the spring of 1947. The islands of the Bikini Atoll and its lagoon would be an uninhabited wasteland for decades after the Able and Baker bomb tests.

The test animals aboard the ships during Test Baker did not fare well, and the results, to the extent shared, could not have offered great solace to the clean-up crews. According to a report in *Time* magazine, "20 pigs were exposed in two shipboard operating rooms. Partially shielded from the bomb's first shower of radiation, they were subjected to a slow cooking from the tons of radioactive water which had soaked the ships. At the end of 14 days all of the Test Baker pigs were dead."[17]

The fate of the crew members who had come aboard the *Arkansas* in the aftermath of the aerial Test Able, including James Elliott and Bill Ringgold, would play out for decades. To quote Elliott, who began undergoing cancer treatments in 1970, "We have been scraped and boiled for over thirty years because of the three weeks we spent trying to clean the contamination from the ship." The U.S. Navy and the Veterans Administration argued for years that any sickness in the men who had boarded the irradiated vessels was not related to exposure from the bomb tests. Eventually, justice prevailed and responsibility was accepted, although too late for some of the sailors.

Similar stories were recorded by other servicemen involved in the cleanup of the irradiated ships. Herbert K. Johnson, now of Port Washington, New York, was assigned as part of the skeleton crew sent to clean up the USS *Fillmore*, which was also anchored in the lagoon. Unlike the *Arkansas*, which was placed a bit closer to the epicenter of the blast, the *Fillmore* managed to stay afloat after both tests. Writing in 2011, Johnson recalled, "After the two atom-bomb tests we were told that our

A live, and seemingly healthy, surgeonfish was captured by the scientists working in the aftermath of the bomb tests. The fish had eaten contaminated algae and absorbed plutonium into its scales, allowing the fish to literally make its own x-ray.

Admiral Blandy, in a confidential report that was later released, stated that "no man was so exposed as to give rise to apprehension that he might become a casualty at a later date." Still, public and private doubts lingered.

ship had not been sunk, or was not severely damaged, and we were given two hours to get her out of the lagoon, since radiation levels were rising at a rapid rate. They neglected to say that when the Baker bomb went off, it splashed the entire ship with radioactive sea-water."

He went on, "We were given no gloves, hats, boots, etc. and no protective clothing and the Geiger counters we were using were making constant noises. The test animals on the ship were partially burned and the plane they put down in the forward hole had been damaged when the deck hatch cover caved in on top of it. Most of the deck rigging and machinery were also all bent out of shape. We were on that ship for another seven months until it was finally decommissioned." Johnson only recently was granted full disability by the VA for the radiation exposure he received as a result of the Bikini bomb tests.[18]

The navy's position that no harm befell any of the 42,000 participants in Operation Crossroads was strongly stated in the months after the bomb tests. Admiral Blandy, in a confidential report that was later released, stated that "no man was so exposed as to give rise to apprehension that he might become a casualty at a later date." Still, public and private doubts lingered.[19]

Ten months after the bomb tests, Navy Secretary James Forrestal ordered that all the servicemen present at Operation Crossroads be given a blood test. What were the results? Despite having been sought in various legal actions over the years, the blood tests given to more than 40,000 men have never been found.[20]

During the 1960s and '70s, hundreds of veterans of the Bikini bomb tests brought claims before the VA for service-related radiation illness, mostly cancer. Lawsuits followed when almost none of the cases were accepted by the VA. Court cases fared little better, in large part because of legislation barring lawsuits against the government for injuries resulting from services in the armed forces. Enough doubt—coupled with compassion—existed, however, that Congress passed a law in 1988 that awarded benefits if the serviceman had a cancer from a specified list, without the need to actually prove a direct link to the radiation exposure.[21]

The damage inflicted on the health of atomic-age veterans began with Bikini, but that was only the start, as the damage would mount in later bomb tests. A December 4, 2011, edition of *Parade* magazine carried a small article titled "Benefits for Vets Exposed to Radiation." The article stated, "The National Association of Atomic Veterans is searching for about 195,000 vets who were exposed to radiation from atmospheric nuclear tests between 1945 and 1962." The article went on to explain that eligible veterans could receive a one-time benefit of $75,000 under the Radiation Exposure

Compensation Act of 1990, or receive a monthly disability payment if they contracted any of twenty-one different cancers known to be related to radiation. Widows and children of those vets who had already died possibly qualified for some of the benefits. Clearly, however, it has taken far too long for Uncle Sam to make it right with the veterans of the atomic age.

A large team of scientists returned to Bikini in the summer of 1947 to run a number of experiments to determine the lingering effects of the two atomic bomb tests. The experiments found the entire area to be "faintly radioactive" but still too dangerous for King Juda and the original native people to return. Dr. Stafford Warren had been the chief of radiological safety at the first atomic bomb test in New Mexico and then at Bikini. His insights seem both naive in parts and wise and far-reaching in others. While stating that the tests proved that radiation penetrates "every crevice," he also stated, "Not one of the 42,000 men who went to Bikini had been detectably injured by radiation." This would prove otherwise, with terrible consequences in later years for many of the men who had gone aboard the *Arkansas* and other ships as cleanup crews. Warren did, however, end his comments with a prophetic statement, "The only defense against atomic bombs still lies outside the scope of science. It is in the prevention of atomic war."[22]

The story of Operation Crossroads would not be complete without a discussion of what became of the Bikinians, the people displaced from their homes before the bomb tests. Prior to 1946, the Bikinians had been a self-sufficient people, living on the rich fishing grounds around their atoll and on farming that fed the fewer than 200 people. Relocated three times, the Bikinians were on the island of Kili by 1948, having almost starved on Rongerik. Unlike the rich diversity the atoll at Bikini had offered, the single island of Kili offered bare subsistence for the tribe over the next two decades. The arrogance of the military toward the displaced people was documented in a 1947 *Saturday Evening Post* article. Carleton Wright, deputy commissioner of the Marshall Islands Trust Territory, was quoted as saying, "Let's not civilize these happy people."[23]

In 1968, President Lyndon Johnson, on the recommendation of advisors that it was now safe, ordered that the Bikinians be resettled on the islands of their atoll. The resettlement occurred in 1969 and lasted until 1978. U.S. medical tests that year revealed that the people had ingested the largest amount of radioactive material of any known population on earth. The immediate removal of the Bikinian people was then ordered. Of the declaration a decade earlier that it was safe to return people to Bikini, Gordon Denning of the Atomic Energy Commission said, "We just plain goofed."[24]

Warren did, however, end his comments with a prophetic statement, "The only defense against atomic bombs still lies outside the scope of science. It is in the prevention of atomic war."

James Elliott (J. D.) and Bill (B. L.) Ringgold posed, along with other crew members, on July 6, 1946, aboard the deck of the Arkansas. The men were all part of a team sent to clean up the damaged, and irradiated, ship after the aerial bomb Test Able exploded. "Cleaning up radiation dust" was the caption on the souvenir photo the men brought home, a photo showing no protective gear in use by men who had apparently been assured there was no danger.

Cleaning up radiation dust on the USS Arkansas BB33 7/6/1946

James Elliott (left) and Bill Ringgold were part of the crew that helped sail the Arkansas to Bikini. After Test Able damaged the ship but did not sink it, the men spent the better part of three weeks cleaning up the radiation dust and debris to prepare the ship for the second bomb, Test Baker. Photo by Ray Hanley; May 2011.

Partial, much delayed, justice finally came in the courts. In 1975, a young attorney, Jonathan M. Weisgall of the Covington & Burling law firm in Washington DC, was assigned the pro bono task of representing the people of Bikini against the U.S. government. Through the tireless work of Weisgall over thirteen years of litigation, a settlement was reached in 1988. The Bikinians were granted a fifteen-year, $75 million settlement of claims for the taking and use of their land. A $110 million trust fund was established for the radiological cleanup and resettlement of Bikini. But the resettlement never occurred.

Ironically, events in the decades after the Bikini Atoll bomb tests would deliver to the state of Arkansas a role in the history of the Marshall Islands quite unrelated to having had its namesake warship being used as a target. Test Able was the first of a total of sixty-seven atomic and hydrogen bombs detonated in the Marshall Islands between 1946 and 1958. The damage took a heavy toll on the once remote Marshallese people who had lived a peaceful life with food aplenty before first the Japanese and then the Americans brought the global war to the idyllic lagoons of their South Pacific home. The United States governed the islands until 1986 when formal independence was granted, while still affording the United States continued military access.

In recognition of the damages inflicted on the islands' environment and economy, the independence compact signed between the islands' government and the United States gave the Marshallese the right to work and live in the United States indefinitely without need of visas. No U.S. citizenship was granted, but the Marshallese were given the right of free travel and freedom to work in the United States.

One lone Marshallese, John Moody, arrived in the late 1980s to work in a Tyson chicken-processing plant in Springdale, Arkansas. Moody sent word back to the Marshall Islands that there were plenty of jobs in northwest Arkansas. The opposite was true back in the islands that were still considered inhabitable (although major health concerns persist), where job seekers outnumbered any available jobs by a reported thirty to one margin.[25]

Today, by far the largest Marshallese population outside the islands calls northwest Arkansas home, and especially Springdale, with more than 4,000 hardworking people who came from the former bomb-targeted islands. By all accounts, these new residents are here to stay. Back home in their native islands there are no jobs, alcoholism afflicts many, and the suicide rate is among the highest in the world. A 2004 U.S. National Cancer Institute study found that the entire island nation was and remains affected by radiation.[26]

Today, by far the largest Marshallese population outside the islands calls northwest Arkansas home, and especially Springdale, with more than 4,000 hardworking people who came from the former bomb-targeted islands. By all accounts, these new residents are here to stay.

We would like to think the site is a shrine to the memory of the thousands of sailors and marines who boarded the Arkansas in the service of the United States of America to help win two world wars and free millions of people from tyranny.

The USS *Arkansas* is still at Bikini, resting mostly upside down in the silt beneath 150 feet of water. The ship, along with the other wrecks at Bikini, has for the past few years been a draw for scuba divers seeking a different type of adventure. We would like to think the site is a shrine to the memory of the thousands of sailors and marines who boarded the *Arkansas* in the service of the United States of America to help win two world wars and free millions of people from tyranny.

The Arkansas *had survived Test Able on July 1, 1946, but it would meet its end on July 25, 1946, with Test Baker, a bomb exploded beneath the sea. The* Arkansas *was reportedly the black dot just to the right of the base of the mushroom plume of sea water that rose a mile into the sky. Before the water could fall back into the sea, the* Arkansas *had already slipped beneath the waves, headed for the bottom of the lagoon. U.S. Navy photo.*

On July 26, 1946, the day after Test Baker, the Arkansas Gazette *carried headlines of the death of the historic warship. The paper also carried this cartoon that reflected on the frightening unknowns of a future in which the power of the atomic bomb could greatly affect the fate of mankind. "Where do we go from here?" was indeed a widely asked question.*

Operation Crossroads was over, deemed (publicly at least) a success by the U.S. Navy. In September 1946, the commander of the Bikini atomic bomb tests, Admiral William H. P. Blandy, celebrated with a mushroom-cloud cake. Blandy—on the left, his wife in the middle—is shown here cutting the celebratory cake. Only in later years would ecological damage and the health impacts to the crew be acknowledged.

Today, the Arkansas rests at the bottom of the lagoon inside the Bikini Atoll in some 150 feet of water. The ship, along with others sunk in the 1946 tests, has in recent years become a draw for scuba divers. This photograph shows one of the big guns on the Arkansas; most of the ship rests topside down, just as it settled to the bottom after sinking within seconds of the bomb blast. Photo used under license by Seawolf Productions.

154

Afterword

The Arkansas nuclear cruiser spent much of its twenty years of service on more or less sentinel duty in and around the Middle East and the Mediterranean. At the time, it was the first nuclear vessel to traverse the Suez Canal.

Some twenty years after the USS *Arkansas* was sunk by an atomic bomb, the U.S. Navy launched a new namesake ship for the state of Arkansas, this one powered by harnessed nuclear energy. The USS *Arkansas* (CGN-41) was the fourth and last ship in the Virginia class of Nuclear-Powered Guided Missile Cruisers. Her keel was laid on January 17, 1977, at Newport News, Virginia, by the Newport News Shipbuilding and Dry Dock Co. Launched on October 21, 1978, she was commissioned three years later, with Captain Dennis S. Read in command.

USS Arkansas CGN-41

The *Arkansas* nuclear cruiser spent much of its twenty years of service on more or less sentinel duty in and around the Middle East and the Mediterranean. At the time, it was the first nuclear vessel to traverse the Suez Canal. The ship was decommissioned and scrapped in 1999, having never fired a shot in combat.

The modern U.S. Navy, an all-volunteer force, is still seen around the world, equipped with satellite and computer technology that would have rendered a surprise attack like the one on Pearl Harbor impossible.

Despite the claims at the time of the 1946 Operation Crossroads bomb tests, the development of atomic weapons did not render the navies of the world obsolete. The modern U.S. Navy, an all-volunteer force, is still seen around the world, equipped with satellite and computer technology that would have rendered a surprise attack like the one on Pearl Harbor impossible.

We would like to think that the first sailors to go to sea on the USS *Arkansas* B-33 in 1912 would be proud of today's generation of American naval servicemen and servicewomen, and at the same time, hope that the sailors of today's U.S. Navy will never forget people like Dave Roberts, Anthony Sirco, "Ace" Elmore, and Homer Ellis—men who helped save the world from tyranny from behind the guns of the oldest ship in the navy fighting across the globe.

Notes

Chapter 1

1. John Spurgeon, "CSS *Arkansas*." *Encyclopedia of Arkansas History & Culture*. http://www.encyclopediaofarkansas.net/encyclopedia/entry-detail.aspx?search=1&entryID=2854.

2. "Missourians Aboard the C.S.S. *Arkansas*." http://www.missouridivision-scv.org/mounits/cssark.htm.

3. Spurgeon, "CSS *Arkansas*."

4. Spurgeon, "CSS *Arkansas*."

5. "Arkansas." http://historycentral.com/navy/CWNavy/Arkansas.html.

6. "USS *Arkansas*/USS *Ozark*," TenderTale. http://www.tendertale.com/tenders/014/014.html.

Chapter 2

1. Captain Roy C. Smith, obituary, *New York Times*, April 12, 1940.

2. Jane M. Hooker, "Willie Kavanaugh Hocker." *Encyclopedia of Arkansas History & Culture*. http://www.encyclopediaofarkansas.net/encyclopedia/entry-detail.aspx?search=1&entryID=2948.

3. History of the USS *Arkansas*, Department of the Navy, Department of Public Information, Washington DC, 1948, 5.

4. *The Archeology of the Atomic Bomb*, chapter three. National Park Service: http://www.nps.gov/history/history/online_books/swcrc/37/chap3.htm.

Chapter 3

1. "Mexican Revolution: Occupation of Veracruz." About.com. http://military-history.about.com/od/battleswars1900s/p/veracruz.htm.

2. History of the USS *Arkansas*, Department of the Navy, Department of Public Information, Washington DC, 1948, p. 5.

3. *Arkansas Democrat*, May 6, 1914.

4. History of the USS *Arkansas*, 5.

Chapter 4

1. "USS Arkansas BB-33." NavyHistory.com. http://www.historycentral.com/navy/battle/Arkansas.html.

2. History of the USS *Arkansas*, Department of the Navy, Department of Public Information, Washington DC, 1948, 3.

3. History of the USS *Arkansas*, 3.

4. History of the USS *Arkansas*, 3.

5. Eugene Wilson, *Comrades of the Mist* (New York: George Sully and Co., 1919).

6. History of the USS *Arkansas*, 3.

Chapter 5

1. History of the USS *Arkansas*, Department of the Navy, Department of Public Information, Washington DC, 1948, 3.

2. History of the USS *Arkansas*, 3.

3. History of the USS *Arkansas*, 3.

4. History of the USS *Arkansas*, 4.

5. History of the USS *Arkansas*, 4.

Chapter 6

1. Ship's Data Section, Office of Public Information, Navy Department, March 1948.

2. Ship's Data Section, March 1948.

3. The Cool Blue Blog, "Omaha Beach and the USS Arkansas." http://coolblue.typepad.com/the_cool_blue_blog/2004/06/omaha_beach_and.html

4. USS *Arkansas*, 1944 Pictorial Review, U.S. Navy, 41.

5. USS *Arkansas*, 1944 Pictorial Review, 41.

6. USS *Arkansas*, 1944 Pictorial Review, 43.

7. The Cool Blue Blog, "Omaha Beach and the USS Arkansas."

8. The Cool Blue Blog, "Omaha Beach and the USS Arkansas."

9. USS *Arkansas*, 1944 Pictorial Review, 43.

10. Ship's Data Section, March 1948.

11. The Cool Blue Blog, "Omaha Beach and the USS Arkansas."

12. Ship's Data Section, March 1948.

13. USS *Arkansas*, 1944 Pictorial Review, 47.

14. Mike Wahrmund, "Remembering the Battleship ARKANSAS," *Sea Classics* 27, no. 2 (February 1994), 16.

15. Wahrmund, "Remembering the Battleship ARKANSAS," 17.

16. Wahrmund, "Remembering the Battleship ARKANSAS," 30.

17. USS *Arkansas*, 1944 Pictorial Review, 49.

18. Michael Ley, "The Saga of America's Oldest Battleship, USS *Arkansas*." *Sea Classics* (January 1998), 61.

19. USS *Arkansas*, 1944 Pictorial Review, 49.

20. Ship's Data Section, March 1948.

21. Ley, "The Saga of America's Oldest Battleship," 61.

22. Wahrmund, "Remembering the Battleship ARKANSAS," 30.

23. Manuscript of Oval Allbritton, Arkansas History Commission, Little Rock, Arkansas.

Chapter 7

1. Lieutenant J. G. "Ace" Fletcher Elmore, obituary, Louisville, Kentucky, *Courier-Journal*, October 16, 2009.

2. Global Security.org, Battle of Okinawa, http://www.globalsecurity.org/military/facility/okinawa-battle.htm

3. Ship's Data Section, Office of Public Information, Navy Department, March 1948.

4. Lieutenant J. G. "Ace" Fletcher Elmore, obituary.

5. *Arklight*, May 25, 1945, 2.

6. Ship's Data Section, March 1948.

7. Ship's Data Section, March 1948.

8. Global Security.org, Battle of Okinawa.

9. Mike Wahrmund, "Remembering the Battleship ARKANSAS," *Sea Classics* 27, no. 2 (February 1994), 46.

10. *Seattle Post-Intelligencer*, October 27, 1945.

11. *Seattle Post-Intelligencer*, October 27, 1945.

12. *Seattle Daily Times*, October 27, 1945, 1.

Chapter 8

1. Jonathan M. Weisgall, *Operation Crossroads: The Atomic Tests at Bikini Atoll* (Annapolis, MD: Naval Institute Press, 1994).

2. Operation Crossroads, Naval History & Heritage Command. http://www.history.navy.mil/faqs/faq76-1.htm.

3. Operation Crossroads, Naval History & Heritage Command.

4. William Blandy, Wikiquotes, http://en.wikiquote.org/wiki/William_H._P._Blandy.

5. Operation Crossroads, Naval History & Heritage Command.

6. Weisgall, *Operation Crossroads*, 140.

7. Weisgall, *Operation Crossroads*, 113.

8. Jack Niedenthal, "Paradise Lost 'for the Good of Mankind.'" *Guardian*, August 6, 2002.

9. Operation Crossroads, Naval History & Heritage Command.

10. Operation Crossroads, Naval History & Heritage Command.

11. Weisgall, *Operation Crossroads*, 156.

12. Weisgall, *Operation Crossroads*, 157.

13. Weisgall, *Operation Crossroads*, 87.

14. Operation Crossroads, Naval History & Heritage Command.

15. Weisgall, *Operation Crossroads*, 222.

16. *Arkansas Democrat*, July 26, 1946, 9.

17. Stafford L. Warren, MD. "What Science Learned at Bikini," *Life*, August 11, 1947, 79.

18. NAVY: National Association of Atomic Veterans, Inc., newsletter, November 2011, 7.

19. Weisgall, *Operation Crossroads*, 268.

20. Weisgall, *Operation Crossroads*, 268.

21. Weisgall, *Operation Crossroads*, 270.

22. Warren, "What Science Learned at Bikini," 88.

23 Weisgall, *Operation Crossroads*, 314.

24. Weisgall, *Operation Crossroads*, 315.

25. Bret Schulte, "For Pacific Islanders, Hopes and Troubles in Arkansas," *New York Times*, July 4, 2012, http://www.nytimes.com/2012/07/05/us/for-marshall-islanders-hopes-and-troubles-in-arkansas.html?hpw&_r=0.

26. Jacqueline Froelich, "Marshallese." *Encyclopedia of Arkansas History & Culture.* http://www.encyclopediaofarkansas.net/encyclopedia/entry-detail.aspx?search=1&entryID=5972.

Bibliography

Interviews

James Elliott, May 15, 2011.

William Ringgold, May 15, 2011.

Jack Freeze, October 31, 2011.

Unpublished Sources

Journals of Anthony Arthur Sirco.

Journals of David Roberts Sr.

Letters of Z. C. Warren, 1918.

Manuscript of Oval Allbritton, Arkansas History Commission, Little Rock, Arkansas.

Oral History Transcripts

Interview of Homer Ellis, MD, conducted by Larry Rabalais, National Museum of the Pacific War, Admiral Nimitz Foundation, Fredericksburg, Texas, February 18, 2005.

Interview of Fletcher "Ace" Elmore, conducted by Joseph W. Ward, Oldham County History Center, Louisville, Kentucky, March 1, 2003.

Books

Parrish, Tom Z. *The Saga of the Confederate Ram Arkansas*. Hillsboro, TX: Hill College Press, 1987.

Still, William N., Jr. *Iron Afloat: The Story of the Confederate Armor-clad.* (1971). Columbia: University of South Carolina Press, 1985.

U.S.S. Arkansas 1944 Pictorial Review, United States Navy, 1944.

Weisgall, Jonathan M. *Operation Crossroads: The Atomic Tests at Bikini Atoll.* Annapolis, MD: Naval Institute Press, 1994.

Wilson, Eugene E. *Comrades of the Mist.* New York: George Sully and Co., 1919.

Wilson, H. A., ed. *U.S.S. Arkansas Pacific War Diary*, United States Navy, 1945.

Other Published Sources

Arkansas Democrat, July 26, 1946.

Arkansas Democrat, May 6, 1914.

Arklight (or *Arklite*), USS *Arkansas* newspaper.

"Benefits for Vets Exposed to Radiation." *Parade*, December 11, 2011.

Bulletin, "Suicide Attacks by Swimmers," March 6, 1945.

Ley, Michael P. "The Saga of America's Oldest Battleship, USS *Arkansas*." *Sea Classics* (January 1998).

Lindley, Ernest K. "Boom and Bust, Bikini." *Newsweek* (July 1, 1946).

NAVY: National Association of Atomic Veterans, Inc., newsletter, November 2011.

New York Times, April 12, 1940.

Niedenthal, Jack. "Paradise Lost 'for the Good of Mankind.'" *Guardian*, August 6, 2002.

Oldenforf, J. B., Vice Admiral, Bulletin, September 6, 1945.

Seattle Daily Times, October 27, 1945, 1.

Ship's Data Section, Office of Public Information, Department of the Navy, History of USS *Arkansas*, March 12, 1948.

"USS Arkansas Battleship," *Arkansas Democrat* Sunday magazine, October 14, 1962, 10.

Wahrmund, Mike. "Remembering the Battleship ARKANSAS." *Sea Classics* 27, no. 2 (February 1994).

Warren, Stafford L., MD. "What Science Learned at Bikini." *Life*, August 11, 1947, 75–87.

Wad, John K. *Twenty-Three Days to Glory: The Saga of the Confederate Ram Arkansas* (Canoga Park, CA: Challenge Publications, Inc.).

Online Sources

Cool Blue Blog: Omaha Beach and the USS *Arkansas*, http://coolblue.typepad.com/the_cool_blue_blog/2004/06/omaha_beach_and.html

Encyclopedia of Arkansas History & Culture, http://www.encyclopediaofarkansas.net/

Global Security.org, Battle of Okinawa, http://www.globalsecurity.org/military/facility/okinawa-battle.htm

HistoryCentral.com, Navy History, http://www.historycentral.com/navy/

MaritimeQuest.com

National Park Service: The Archeology of the Atomic Bomb, http://www.nps.gov/history/history/online_books/swcrc/37/

Naval History & Heritage Command, http://www.history.navy.mil/index.html

NavSource Naval History, http://www.navsource.org

Steelnavy.com

Index

Anderson, Captain Edward, 36

Annapolis, Maryland, 58

Arklight 56, 57, 58, 65 ,67, 112, 119

Atlantic Fleet, 28

Atomic Energy Commission, 149

Baton Rouge, Louisiana, 16, 17

Blandy, Admiral William, 131, 132, 133, 135, 136, 147, 148, 154

Bonanza, Arkansas 59

Bronson, Captain Amon, 57

Brough, Charles, 56

Brown, Isaac, 15

Bryant, Captain Carleton 60, 87, 94, 99

Bullard, Captain W. H., 45

Camden, New Jersey, 22

Casco Bay, Maine, 60, 83, 86

CSS *Arkansas*, 15, 16, 17, 18

Daniels, Josephus, 29, 42, 47, 63

Daughters of the American Revolution, 20

Denning, Gordon, 149

DeWeese, Captain Wade, 129, 137

Dewey, Admiral George, 44

Dimes, Joe, 58

Eisenhower, Dwight, 88

Elliott, James 137, 139, 140, 141, 142, 143, 144, 147, 150

Ellis, Dr. Homer, 114, 115, 116, 120, 126, 156

Elmore, J. G. Fletcher "Ace," 111, 112, 118, 125, 156

Fletcher, Admiral Frank, 36

Forrestal, James 48

Freeze, Jack, 143, 146

Fried, Louis, 37, 39

Gloeckle, A. H., 53

Grady, Lieutenant John, 36, 37

Greenrock, Scotland, 58

Guantanamo, Cuba, 44, 59, 69

Hall, Ethel, 45, 53

Hampton Roads, Virginia, 37, 44, 59, 72

Hancock, Orville, 93

Harris, Samuel, 16

Havana, Cuba, 70, 71

Herz, William, 48

Hiroshima, 122

Hitler, Adolf, 59, 88, 90, 101

Hocker, Willie, 20

Hodges, Earl, 20

Hoover, Herbert, 58, 72, 74

Huerta, Victoriana 35, 38

Ingram, Lieutenant Jonas, 37, 41

Iwo Jima, 110, 112, 114, 115, 116, 117, 120, 124

Johnson, Herbert K., 147

Johnson, Lyndon, 149

Keating, Lieutenant Arthur, 37

Kelly, Richard, 85, 89, 90, 92

Key West, Florida, 25

Kiel, Germany, 76

King Juda, 133

Konosky, Peter Paul, 128

Krock, Arthur, 130

Laney, Ben, 123

Laurence, William, 145

Leyte Gulf, 122

MacArthur Museum of Arkansas
    Military History, 66

Macon, Nancy 20, 23

Macon, Robert, 20, 23

Madero, Francisco, 35

Marshall Islands, 133, 151

Mayo, Henry, 35

McLean, Captain Ridley, 68

McMahon, Brien, 131

Memphis, Tennessee, 13

Moffett, Admiral William, 73

Monfort, Aurelio, 36

Moody, John, 151

Moore, McFarlane, 73

Motor World, 49

Mount Suribachi, 112, 116, 117

Nagasaki, 122

Naples, Italy, 26, 58

National Association of Atomic
    Veterans, 148

National Cancer Institute, 135,
    151

New York Naval Yard, 57

Newport, Rhode Island, 44

Nice, France, 58

Nimtz, Chester, 82

Norfolk, Virginia, 61, 86

Okinawa, 102, 116, 117, 118,
    119, 120, 122, 123, 124, 126,
    128, 129

Omaha Beach, 93, 94, 106, 107

Operation Crossroads, 130, 131,
    132, 134, 141, 143, 148, 149,
    154, 156

Osburn, F. C., 29

Oslo, Norway, 58

Panama Canal, 21, 25, 57, 58, 59,
    61, 62, 68, 106, 110, 123

Pearl Harbor, 86, 156

Petain, Henre, 74

Philadelphia Naval Yard, 20, 22,
    24, 57

Plymouth, England, 58

Porter, Phillip, 145

Read, Captain Dennis, 155

Reykjavik, Iceland, 60

Richards, Captain Frederick, 83,
    84, 90, 105

Ringgold, Bill, 137, 139, 140, 141,
    143, 144, 147, 150

Roberts, David, 84, 87, 92, 93,95,
    99, 101, 102, 103, 156

Robinson, D. S., 121

Roosevelt, Franklin D., 58, 60, 121

Rosyth, Scotland, 45

Rush, William, 36

Sawmiller, R. B., 70, 79, 80, 81, 82

Scientific American magazine, 33

Seattle, Washington, 123, 129

Sirco, Anthony, 84, 85, 87, 93, 94,
    95, 97, 98, 99, 100, 101, 102,
    103, 110, 111, 114, 119, 120,
    121, 122, 128, 129, 156

Slotin, Louis, 132

Smith, Captain Roy, 20, 26, 42

SMS Schleswig-Holstein, 76

Strauss, Lewis, 131

Springdale, Arkansas, 151

Taft, William H., 21, 25

Tampico, Mexico, 36

Tarawa, 88

Truman, Harry, 132

USS *Alabama*, 130

USS *Augusta*, 60

USS *Dolphin*, 36

USS *Fillmore*, 147

USS *Florida*, 20

USS *Nevada*, 99, 144

USS *New Hampshire*, 36

USS *New York*, 21

USS *Ozark*, 18

USS *Rockbridge*, 134, 137, 144

USS *Texas*, 20, 59, 106, 130

Van Dorn, Earl, 16

Veracruz, Mexico, 36, 38, 39, 41, 42, 88

Vicksburg, Mississippi, 16, 17

Wabbaseka, Arkansas, 20

Warren, Dr. Stafford, 149

Warren, Z. C., 27, 45, 46, 47, 53

Watson, William, 37, 39

Weisgall, Jonathan, 151

Wilson, Woodrow, 25, 35, 36, 38, 39, 44, 47

Winslow, Admiral Cameron, 26

Wright, Carleton, 149

Wyatt, Ben, 133

Zaragoza, Ignacio, 35